MW01531687

Southern Methodist University

Dallas, Texas

Written by Stacy M. Seebode

Edited by Kelly Carey and Kristine Rodriguez

Layout by Kimberly Moore

*Additional contributions by Omid Gohari,
Christina Koshzow, Chris Mason, Joey Rahimi,
and Luke Skurman*

COLLEGE PROWLER®

ISBN # 1-4274-0133-0
© Copyright 2006 College Prowler
All Rights Reserved
Printed in the U.S.A.
www.collegeprowler.com

Last updated 5/15/06

Special Thanks To: Babs Carryer, Andy Hannah, Launch-Cyte, Tim O'Brien, Bob Sehlinger, Thomas Emerson, Andrew Skurman, Barbara Skurman, Bert Mann, Dave Lehman, Daniel Fayock, Chris Babyak, The Donald H. Jones Center for Entrepreneurship, Terry Slease, Jerry McGinnis, Bill Ecenberger, Idie McGinty, Kyle Russell, Jacque Zaremba, Larry Winderbaum, Roland Allen, Jon Reider, Team Evankovich, Lauren Varacalli, Abu Noaman, Mark Exler, Daniel Steinmeyer, Jared Cohon, Gabriela Oates, David Koegler, and Glen Meakem.

Bounce-Back Team: Tommy Newton, Chris Noon, and Kristen Germain.

College Prowler®
5001 Baum Blvd.
Suite 750
Pittsburgh, PA 15213

Phone: 1-800-290-2682
Fax:1-800-772-4972
E-Mail: info@collegeprowler.com
Web Site: www.collegeprowler.com

Welcome to College Prowler®

During the writing of College Prowler's guidebooks, we felt it was critical that our content was unbiased and unaffiliated with any college or university. We think it's important that our readers get honest information and a realistic impression of the student opinions on any campus—that's why if any aspect of a particular school is terrible, we (unlike a campus brochure) intend to publish it. While we do keep an eye out for the occasional extremist—the cheerleader or the cynic—we take pride in letting the students tell it like it is. We strive to create a book that's as representative as possible of each particular campus. Our books cover both the good and the bad, and whether the survey responses point to recurring trends or a variation in opinion, these sentiments are directly and proportionally expressed through our guides.

College Prowler guidebooks are in the hands of students throughout the entire process of their creation. Because you can't make student-written guides without the students, we have students at each campus who help write, randomly survey their peers, edit, layout, and perform accuracy checks on every book that we publish. From the very beginning, student writers gather the most up-to-date stats, facts, and inside information on their colleges. They fill each section with student quotes and summarize the findings in editorial reviews. In addition, each school receives a collection of letter grades (A through F) that reflect student opinion and help to represent contentment, prominence, or satisfaction for each of our 20 specific categories. Just as in grade school, the higher the mark the more content, more prominent, or more satisfied the students are with the particular category.

Once a book is written, additional students serve as editors and check for accuracy even more extensively. Our bounce-back team—a group of randomly selected students who have no involvement with the project—are asked to read over the material in order to help ensure that the book accurately expresses every aspect of the university and its students. This same process is applied to the 200-plus schools College Prowler currently covers. Each book is the result of endless student contributions, hundreds of pages of research and writing, and countless hours of hard work. All of this has led to the creation of a student information network that stretches across the nation to every school that we cover. It's no easy accomplishment, but it's the reason that our guides are such a great resource.

When reading our books and looking at our grades, keep in mind that every college is different and that the students who make up each school are not uniform—as a result, it is important to assess schools on a case-by-case basis. Because it's impossible to summarize an entire school with a single number or description, each book provides a dialogue, not a decision, that's made up of 20 different topics and hundreds of student quotes. In the end, we hope that this guide will serve as a valuable tool in your college selection process. Enjoy!

OMID GOHARI ○ CHRISTINA KOSHZOW ○ CHRIS MASON ○ JOEY RAHIMI ○ LUKE SKURMAN ○
The College Prowler Team

Table of Contents

Introduction from the Author

When people ask me what attracted me to SMU, I can't help but giggle on the inside because initially, I disliked the school. On my first visit, no one talked to me except the other prospective students and my tour guide. It didn't seem like a friendly atmosphere filled with southern hospitality at first glance. After I was rejected by my first choice, SMU started to look appealing for several reasons: location, programs, and size. If it had not been for two girls from my hometown that happened to come here, I would not be here, for I had never even heard of SMU.

Several students will shrug their shoulders when you ask them why they chose SMU, but all of them will proudly boast about what a great school it is. After planting my roots here for the last three years, I can finally see what all the hype is about. SMU is an awesome school, and for some it takes time for them to realize it. SMU obviously has areas that need improvement, but that can be said about any school.

SMU is a place where you can explore your career options without having to transfer to another school for a different major. Whether or not you are social by nature, this school teaches you the skills to become gregarious. You have the chance to speak up in class and have the teacher respond to you by name. SMU has excellent study abroad programs in about twenty different countries, as well as a program in Washington D.C. with American University. The options at this school are endless. You can also get involved with any of the 200-plus organizations on campus.

SMU may not be the most racially diverse school in the nation; however, SMU conquers that category in terms of general diversity. There are students here from all different types of financial backgrounds. A majority of the students, rich or poor, are here on scholarship, thanks to SMU's generous donors. SMU is also very conservative, but as I have learned, conservative or not, meeting people of assorted backgrounds is the best way to become well-rounded. And it might just make you learn something new about yourself in the process.

If you're curious about SMU, I would advise you to come, take a tour of the campus, and make a point to talk to students. They are the best sources. The statistical information is available online, but you should experience SMU for yourself and see if this is the place where you can spread your wings for the next four years. Hopefully, this book can point you in the right direction, wherever that may be.

Stacy M. Seebode, Author
Southern Methodist University

By the Numbers

General Information

Southern Methodist University
6425 Boaz Lane
Dallas, TX 75205

Control:
Private

Academic Calendar:
Semester

Religious Affiliation:
United Methodist

Founded:
1911

Web Site:
www.smu.edu

Main Phone:
(214) 768-2000

Admissions Phone:
(214) 768-2058

Student Body

Full-Time Undergraduates:
5,882

Part-Time Undergraduates:
362

Total Male Undergraduates:
2,795

Total Female Undergraduates:
3,413

Admissions

Overall Acceptance Rate:
64%

Regular Acceptance Rate:
64%

Total Applicants:
6,434

Total Acceptances:
4,136

Freshman Enrollment:
1,313

Yield (% of admitted students who actually enroll):
32%

Early Decision Available?
No

Early Action Available?
Yes

Early Action Deadline:
November 1

Early Action Decision Notification:
December 31

Regular Decision Deadline:
March 15

Regular Decision Notification:
Rolling

Must-Reply-By Date:
May 1

Applicants Placed on Waiting List:
682

Applicants Accepted from Waiting List:
345

Students Enrolled from Waiting List:
93

Transfer Applications Received:
697

Transfer Applications Accepted:
465

Transfer Students Enrolled:
295

Common Application Accepted?
Yes

Supplemental Forms?
No

Admissions E-Mail:
ugadmission@smu.edu

Admissions Web Site:
www.smu.edu/admission

SAT I or ACT Required?
Either

SAT II Requirements?
Only for home-schooled Students

First-Year Students Submitting SAT Scores:
79%

→

**SAT I Range
(25th–75th Percentile):**
1110–1300

**SAT I Verbal Range
(25th–75th Percentile):**
550–640

**SAT I Math Range
(25th–75th Percentile):**
560–660

Retention Rate:
87%

**Top 10% of High
School Class:**
36%

Application Fee:
$50

Financial Information

Tuition:
$26,880

Room and Board:
$9,307

Books and Supplies:
$600

**Average Need-Based
Financial Aid Package
(including loans, work-study,
grants, and other sources):**
$22,973

**Students Who Applied for
Financial Aid:**
46%

Students Who Received Aid:
39%

**Financial Aid Forms
Deadline:**
February 15

Financial Aid Phone:
(214) 768-3016

Financial Aid E-Mail:
enrol_serv@main.smu.edu

Financial Aid Web Site:
www.smu.edu/financial_aid

Academics

The Lowdown On...
Academics

Degrees Awarded:
Bachelor
Master
Professional
Doctorate
Certificate
Post-Bachelor Certificate

Most Popular Majors:
28% Business Management
16% Social Sciences
12% Communication
10% Psychology
 8% Visual/Performing Arts

Undergraduate Schools:
Cox School of Business
Dedman College of Humanities and Sciences
Dedman School of Law
Meadows School of the Arts
Perkins School of Theology
School of Engineering

Full-Time Faculty:
576

Faculty with Terminal Degree:
84%

Student-to-Faculty Ratio:
12:1

Average Course Load:
4–5 Classes

Graduation Rates:
Four-Year: 56%
Five-Year: 69%
Six-Year: 71%

Special Degree Options

Markets and Culture Interdisciplinary major, Co-op program in Engineering School, two evening degrees in Humanities and Social Sciences

AP /IB Test Score Requirements

AP - Possible advanced placement for scores of 4 or 5
IB - Possible advanced placement for scores of 5, 6, or 7

Best Places to Study

Fondren Library Center, Bridwell Library, Hamon Arts Library, residence hall study rooms

Sample Academic Clubs

Advertising Club, Anthropology Club, Black Law Students Association, Chemistry Society, Debate and Forensics Society, Political Science Symposium, Russian Club, SMU Amateur Radio Club, Society of Women Engineers, Spanish Club

Did You Know?

SMU features a **Tate Lecture Series** every year, where students are given the chance to listen to honored and celebrated guest speakers. Past guests have been Bill O'Reilly, John Irving, Dick Cheney, Sidney Poitier, Jane Goodall, Julie Andrews, Ted Turner, Tom Brokaw, and many more. Recent line-ups included: Bob Dole, Al Gore, Wade Davis, and Barbara Walters.

The Meadows Museum is home to the largest and most inclusive **collection of Spanish art** outside of Spain. Some of the original works by El Greco, Velázquez, Ribera, Murillo, Goya, Miró, and Picasso are all showcased here.

The "Campaign for SMU: A Time to Lead" **raised over $532 million for educational needs**, campus construction, and renovations over a period of five years. In September of 2005, the first phase of renovations to the Dedman Center for Lifetime Sports was completed and features two basketball courts, an extended track, a climbing wall, swimming facilities, indoor soccer, and much more. Also, in 2005, construction of a new business education building was completed. SMU has a substantial amount of funding to maintain the beauty of its campus.

"Most of the teachers I have had are really good. They have a lot of real world experience, which makes classes much more interesting."

Q "Quite honestly, I've only found **two professors that are interesting**."

Q "The teachers are very different. **Each teacher has their own distinctive teaching style and mission** to get across in class, unlike high school where teachers are shackled to get certain curriculum taken care of. This is both a blessing and a curse because you might have two teachers teaching the same class where one teacher grades harder than the other, but you may learn more from the other teacher. This freedom creates an environment where you will find the best teachers. Well, that depends—once again, the strength of the teacher really affects the class more so than the class itself. I had one teacher that made me enthusiastic about the class because of her excitement about the class, not the content. Classes are heavily affected based on the teacher. And most teachers want to be there, so you win on that side, too. Classes are so small that you get the chance to get to know your professors."

Q "Almost all professors I have come in contact with are very helpful and attentive to their students. So far, **classes have been interesting**; however, I think that a lot of that depends on the student's willingness to apply him or herself in combination with the professor and subject matter."

Q "I find most of the **professors here to be very sharp and on task in the classroom**. Besides being very intelligent, most professors are also easy to confront with concerns, or to just have a friendly chat with. I believe a class only to be as interesting as the professor who teaches it. All my classes in the political science and Italian department are challenging, yet all the classes have an environment that is conducive to learning but also fun to be in."

Q "Teachers vary. The majority of my classes were interesting, except English and history. Teachers whom I enjoyed were **really enthusiastic about their work**."

Q "Most of the teachers here are awesome. On the whole, they enjoy teaching. **My classes are intriguing**, but that usually rests on the professor. If the professor can communicate something as boring as calculus in an interesting and relevant manner, then I will enjoy it."

Q "The teachers are great. Although **way too many of them do not speak English well enough** for an hour and a half of pure lecture. Overall, the classes are very interesting, especially when you get all of the boring prerequisites out of the way."

Q "The first year, I didn't think the classes were that interesting because we were required to take lots of general education classes. However, **once I declared my major, I got to take the classes that really appealed to me**. As for the teachers, all of mine have been really fair and understanding. They completely understand if you get sick and have to miss a class. All of them have been willing to help me and let me come by during their office hours."

Q "Most of the teachers I've found so far are pretty boring. The teacher really defines the class. The classes that I've had that were boring had boring teachers. **No teachers really stick out in my mind as being phenomenal**."

Q "Most teachers in beginning level classes are nice but not very personal. **Once you are in a major-oriented class, then the teachers can have fun** and make what you are learning lively. They are definitely more personal and much more willing to help outside of class. They remember your name and most are available all the time."

Q "SMU has a great reputation, but **I really don't think the classes are that much harder than Texas Tech**, even though we are supposed to be so much better. I think we just have better PR. SMU is not the 'Harvard of the South,' or whatever the saying is."

Q "In the University Honors Program at SMU, professors are very engaging in the classrooms, a lot of reading is required, and students do a lot of papers. **Along with the small size of classes comes an intimate setting** inside the classroom and a close relationship with professors outside the classroom. I have found this to be very beneficial. For example, I can get coffee with any of my professors to talk about materials in class, or maybe just talk about other interests. This makes class so much more interactive and very interesting; not like a lecture at all."

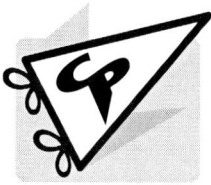

The College Prowler Take On...
Academics

It is obvious that sometime in your college career, you will encounter the teacher that everyone has been avoiding. There is no way to dodge that ball. SMU can make no guarantees, just like any other institution, but at least they offer a number of intelligent professors that are interesting. Most are either here to continue research or have already attained their doctorate. The likelihood that you will encounter a boring teacher is quite low. Students tend to agree that your class is as stimulating as you make it. SMU professors are enthusiastic about their subject matter as well as friendly. Every professor is required to post office hours, but most will go out of their way after an arduous day to make sure that every one of their students' questions—even the most mundane—are answered. I have had several professors that allowed me to call them at home or have worked around my schedule. Even the most stringent professors secretly cheer for you in the shadows.

The courses are noteworthy and challenging enough to force you to find the library. Some professors are lenient with assignments while others make you feel as though you are already in law school. SMU teachers are very strict on one thing in particular though: attendance. The well-known phrase at SMU is "Go to Class!" Adhere to it or watch your grade slowly plummet to its death. At SMU, you can feel confident knowing that at any time you can change majors without having to change schools. Every program here is in high regard nationwide and is constantly being enhanced. Most students say that the academics become harder every year—so be prepared to lose sleep.

B+

The College Prowler® Grade on
Academics: B+

A high Academics grade generally indicates that professors are knowledgeable, accessible, and genuinely interested in their students' welfare. Other determining factors include class size, how well professors communicate, and whether or not classes are engaging.

Local Atmosphere

The Lowdown On...
Local Atmosphere

Region:
South

City, State:
Dallas, Texas

Setting:
Urban

Distance to Austin:
3 hours

Distance to Houston:
4 hours

Points of Interest:
American Airlines Center
Ameriquest Field
The Dallas Museum of Art
The Dallas World Aquarium
Hurricane Harbor
Lone Star Park
The Meyerson
Music Hall at Fair Park
Six Flags over Texas
Smirnoff Music Centre
The Texas Motor Speedway

→

Closest
Movie Theaters:

Angelika Film Center at
Mockingbird Station
5321 E. Mockingbird Lane
(214) 841-4700

Loews At Cityplace
2600 N. Haskell Ave.
(214) 828-6008

The Magnolia at
West Village
3699 E. McKinney Ave.
(214) 764-9106

Regent at Highland
Park Village
32 Highland Park Village
(214) 526-9668

Closest
Shopping Malls:

The Galleria
Highland Park Village
Mockingbird Station
NorthPark Center
West Village

Major Sports Teams:

Cowboys (football)
Rangers (baseball)
Stars (hockey)
Burn (soccer)

City Web Sites

www.dallascvb.com/visitors
www.dallascityhall.com
www.dallas.com

Did You Know?

5 Fun Facts about Dallas:

- Dallas ranks as the **ninth largest city** in the U.S.
- The **State Fair of Texas** has been held every year since 1886 in the same location: Fair Park.
- *Dallas*, the television show that ran for 13 years, featured the Dallas area.
- CBS's *Walker Texas Ranger*, was filmed in Dallas.
- With more than **13,000 births per year**, the Dallas Parkland Hospital System is the largest birthing center in the country. Oooh, baby!

Famous People from Dallas:

Jensen Ackles

Erykah Badu

Ernie Banks

Clyde Barrow

William Ramsey Clark

Emily Erwin

Martie Erwin

Morgan Fairchild

Melinda Gates

Peri Gilpin

Angie Harmon

Norah Jones

George McFarland

Meatloaf

Tracy Needham

Aaron Spelling

Stevie Ray Vaughan

Owen Wilson

Robin Wright-Penn

Local Slang:

Ya'll – Southern way of saying "you all" or "you guys"

Blows – Another word for sucks or stinks; "this blows"

Izzle – This is attached to everything, mostly by guys

Fixin' – Southern way of saying "about to" or "fixing to"

Students Speak Out On...
Local Atmosphere

"It's Dallas! A huge city with lots of money. Like all cities, stay away from unsafe areas and be sure to experience the arts—theater, musicals, symphony, and museums."

Q "Dallas is a lot of fun, although **it is very segregated**. You can be in one area with nice people and cars and then cross into a new place with dangerous people."

Q "The atmosphere is **better for natives than for international students**."

Q "It is a very nice atmosphere located in the Park Cities because it is a **well-to-do area of Dallas**. We're the only real university in the area. That's nice because we don't have to compete with any other schools. There are a lot of communities, families, and apartments. There are plenty of concerts, restaurants, bars, music venues, and festivals. Then you drive south for two minutes and you get robbed. Definitely know where you're going, especially if it's at night. If you're planning on going to a new area by yourself, don't go. It may be known as the number one crime city right now, but at least it isn't violent crime. Unlike some cities, there are a lot of fantastic things in Dallas. You take the good with the bad."

Q "Dallas has a lot of things to do, especially if you seek them out. There are various arts venues and decent shows and exhibits. **There are several other universities in the general Dallas-Ft. Worth area**, though I have yet to come into direct contact with any students from other schools."

Q "Dallas is a great city. There is a lot to do around campus, although for a lot of it, you must be 21 or older. Also, the people in Dallas are usually very friendly and pleasant. **Driving in Dallas can be complicated, but most people around here are very courteous drivers**. There are other universities around the Dallas/Fort Worth area, but you don't hear much from them unless we are competing with them in athletics. Definitely visit the Dallas World Aquarium and Greenville Avenue. Stay away from Deep Ellum if you're alone—and especially if you are a female by yourself. It is pretty safe, however, when there are parties there that you can get bused to."

Q "The atmosphere in Dallas is vast. **It is a fast-paced, big city, but it still keeps the pride and character of Texas**. There are universities around, but I haven't had much interaction with them. As with any big city, stay away from the sketchy parts of town and the strip-clubs. Visit all the landmarks of Dallas: the museums, art galleries, historic monuments—anything you can get into your sight, go see it."

Q "Dallas is a great college city. There are tons of restaurants and bars, and there is plenty to do on the weekends. **If you are into the party scene, you can't go wrong with Greenville Avenue**. It is so close to campus, and Deep Ellum is right downtown."

Q "**Dallas isn't really a college town**. You don't have the dives that most other college kids go to. I would say that the local atmosphere lacks some of the college cheapness."

Q "SMU is in Dallas, which is a big city, however, there is always a lot to do on campus, so **it feels like you're always seeing someone you know when you walk through campus** to class. TCU is about an hour away, but no one really goes over there."

Q "The atmosphere is great. I have lived in a suburb not too far from SMU my whole life, so the atmosphere has not really changed all that much. **There are many universities around**. I have many friends that go to TCU, UNT, and many other community colleges. On the matter of what to stay away from, that would definitely be an area for common sense. We all know better than to walk by ourselves in an unfamiliar place."

Q "I think it's a great city to have a school in—large enough so you have a city feeling, and not like you're in the middle of nowhere. **SMU is active in the community and receives a lot of positive support from it**. The city has a lot of character and diversity with lots to do (I, however, stay on campus mostly). Dallas features a great day life and night life. The school is in the best part of town. There is something here for everyone."

Q "The atmosphere is great, even though **it can sometimes be considered a bubble**. People are very nice and approachable. There are no universities around. The local area is reasonably safe, so there is not much to stay away from. Places to visit: Lower Greenville, Deep Ellum, and Highland Park, which is located three minutes from campus."

Q "Highland Park is an upscale residential neighborhood, and the attitude of its citizens directly reflects on the university. Students feel the pressure of the wealthy community as well as the feel of a prosperous urban downtown district. **Dallas has a lot of history, and the campus museum is among the best collections in its class**."

Q "The city of University Park is **very upscale and suburban**. Some of the benefits are a really low number of crimes and a very eye-pleasing background for after-class activities. The disadvantages are the traffic, pollution, and lack of support for the school's failing football program."

Q "I love Dallas, but I've also lived here my entire life. I remember my freshman year, people would say that they hated Dallas, and I never understood why. It is pretty upscale around here. **People walk around with their noses in the air and are very prissy**. I would definitely stay away from South Dallas, places like Oak Cliff, that's where all the gangs hang out. I love that Dallas has so many professional sports teams. You can go see any of their games."

The College Prowler Take On...
Local Atmosphere

To the non-Dallasonian, this city may seem like nothing but tall cowboy boots and hats. But, if anything, Dallas breeds sophisticated cowboys. When I say cowboys, I am not referring to the ones that ride horses and chew on hay; I am alluding to the polite and sociable ones. By the time you are ready to graduate, you will have the best handle on the ins and outs of the city; however, at that point, it will be time for your departure. But for now, you have four years to explore. SMU is located in the midst of the Park Cities, which is comprised of University Park and Highland Park. Both areas are the wealthiest ones in Dallas. The best aspect of this area is its safety. The community is one similar to *Pleasantville*, where everyone knows everyone. And it is true, there is something here for everyone. The neatest thing about Dallas is that it features live music every night of the week, most of which will be found in Deep Ellum. The museums and Fair Park constantly feature new works of art.

There is always something to do, and everything is at your fingertips—if you have a car. The shopping and dining scenes in Dallas are among the most prestigious places in the nation (San Francisco, New York, Miami, Beverly Hills). Dallas is the home of several top sports teams. Not only do you have the best of what's around, but if you're low on cash, you can still find something amusing to do on any given day. White Rock Lake is a mere five minutes from campus if you're in the mood for a bike ride or a jog. Of course, everyone is aware of the crime rate here. Just as with any other urban city, the best thing to do is to use common sense. Do not embark on a journey into new territory unless it is with a friend. With all that said, I am still finding little treasures in the most remote parts of the city.

The College Prowler® Grade on

Local Atmosphere: A-

A high Local Atmosphere grade indicates that the area surrounding campus is safe and scenic. Other factors include nearby attractions, proximity to other schools, and the town's attitude toward students.

Safety & Security

The Lowdown On...
Safety & Security

Number of SMU Police:
22

Police Phone:
Emergency
(214) 768-3333

Non-emergency
(214) 768-3388

Safety Services:
Blue-lights (emergency phones)

Campus security escort program

E-mails about campus alerts

"Giddy Up" carts

Line of Defense (self-defense class)

"The Seven Steps to Personal Safety" program

→

Health Services:

Allergies

Consultations with physicians

Counseling services

Injuries

Immunizations

Minor surgery

On-campus pharmacy

Specialty clinics (dental consultation, dermatology, gynecology, orthopedics, and sports medicine)

Treatment for minor illnesses

Health Center Office Hours:

Monday–Friday
8:30 a.m.–5 p.m.

Did You Know?

Dallas wins the gold medal with the **highest crime rate in the United States**, consisting of primarily burglaries and robberies. The city has consistently been ranked in the top ten for nearly a decade.

SMU recently created a program, "Giddy Up," where students can call and have **volunteer students come pick them up** in a golf cart and get a safe ride home. This is to prevent students from driving under the influence. If you are intoxicated, don't be afraid to simply call.

Students Speak Out On...
Safety & Security

"You always see the cops on campus. They are only a phone call or blue box away. But, you should still use common sense. Don't walk in dark or sketchy areas. Robberies and other incidents do happen."

Q "I always feel very safe. **There aren't really any outsiders or intruders on this campus**."

Q "Ninety percent **good**."

Q "I have heard of some instances of car jacking and minor theft, but besides that, the campus, from my perspective, has been **a very safe place to be, even at night**."

Q "**SMU has its very own police department**, which seems to be a rarity on most campuses. Security is taken very seriously here because of its proximity to Dallas. There are several safety zones and police cars on patrol."

Q "The security here is top of the line. If there is ever an emergency, there are **blue boxes all over the campus**, and a police officer will come to you immediately."

Q "Safety and security is good. Only minor incidents occur and **there are always campus patrol officers driving around**."

Q "It's all pretty good. I haven't had many problems, but **we have had girls raped and students robbed**. I have never felt unsafe, though."

Q "Well, it really depends on who you ask. Personally, **I have never had a problem with security**. But then again, my friends and I don't go walking off by ourselves in the middle of the night."

Q "There are blue campus security buttons all over, so if you feel unsafe, help will arrive immediately. Also, **the campus is well lit**. I have had no problems with safety—I've walked on campus alone at night many times and have never felt threatened. The security is in such excess that sometimes it's ridiculous. The Student Senate Student Issues Committee actually meets once a semester with the police department and other school officials to do the Light the Night walk, where they walk the entire campus and note the places that need more light or even a blue security light."

Q "I think security is pretty good; **I always see SMU police driving around campus**. However, there are a lot of places on campus that are not that well lit, which can be a little scary when walking back from a night class or back to your dorm/apartment."

Q "Safety is good, even though there have been a few incidents over the years. They do not occur too often. Security is good, meaning that it doesn't keep you down. **You don't see cops everywhere, but you know they are patrolling**. That is pretty reassuring."

Q "**I do not feel safe at night alone**. There have been violent attacks with little apparent police action. I travel in groups or by car."

Q "They're **more worried about giving parking tickets** than stopping people from getting on campus that shouldn't be. I feel somewhat safe, but you always hear stories about people getting held up at gunpoint. It makes you look behind you when you're walking at night."

Q "**Safety was an issue on campus**, but I think it is getting better. The police department has taken a lot of heat, so I think they will do better in the future."

The College Prowler Take On...
Safety & Security

SMU may boast a very safe campus; however, they should really say thank you to University Park. Even though University Park and SMU Police work together to patrol the city, SMU PD pays more attention to parking violations than a screaming girl whose hair is in flames. On the other hand, nothing too out of the ordinary ever occurs here on campus, so what else is there for them to do? It is quite rare to hear about SMU students being mugged at gunpoint. There have only been two incidents since I have been here, and both of them were off-campus. A friend of mine was raped when she was a freshman. So, if you receive warnings from anyone, especially if you are a female, it will probably pertain to rape. There are several minor thefts reported every year, but there is nothing to fear on this campus—except a parking ticket.

Most of the police force here are fairly friendly and do earnestly look out for you, especially if you are intoxicated. I hear more about alcohol violations than Sherlock Holmes murder mysteries. SMU has done a stellar job with the PR for their police force, and I definitely commend them for that. I have yet to see an SMU cop put to the test, though. So, that should really give you a good idea about the campus: it's safe enough.

B-

The College Prowler® Grade on

Safety & Security: B-

A high grade in Safety & Security means that students generally feel safe, campus police are visible, blue-light phones and escort services are readily available, and safety precautions are not overly necessary.

Computers

The Lowdown On...
Computers

High-Speed Network?
Yes

Wireless Network?
Yes

Number of Labs:
5

Number of Computers:
409

Operating Systems:
Windows and Mac

Free Software

Adobe Acrobat Reader, SMU PPP-Windows, Internet Explorer 6.0 (includes SP1), Virus Stingers, McAfee Virus Definitions, IE 5.1.6, SMU PPP-Ethernet Applications

Discounted Software

McAfee Antivirus: $10
Windows XP Pro Upgrade: $99

24-Hour Labs

Hughes-Trigg Student Center, first floor

Charge to Print?

Yes

Did You Know?

SMU has an agreement with AT&T personal wireless services as well as Resicom where students can receive extra minutes, **discounts on their cell phones** and bills, as well as long distance calling cards.

ITS (Information Technology Services) will assist you in **developing your own Web site** and provides several references for extra guidance.

SMU has its own computer store (Computer Corner) where **students can purchase hardware** as well as software—all at discounted rates.

Images, located on campus, is solely a place for printing needs. Recently, it expanded its services to include QuickPrint, where **students can submit copy orders online** without the hassle of using a telephone.

Students Speak Out On...
Computers

"Computers are always available in the libraries. However, during exam time, the labs are pretty crowded, and you will want your own computer."

Q "Bring your own computer. **Computer areas are available, but in dorms they are not updated** and in the union it is always crowded with people using them. Libraries have a lot of computers but are not open all the time. It is much more convenient to have your own computer. I recommend a laptop, because you are always on the go and a portable computer is much easier."

Q "**You have to have your own computer**. Computer labs are not very accessible. We have good equipment, though."

Q "It depends on the time and place in reference to whether or not the computer labs are crowded. **I would recommend bringing your own computer** if at all possible—just for ease and flexibility of writing, editing, papers, and Internet use."

Q "I think going into college, you should have your own computer in the first place, but if that is not an option, the computer labs and facilities at SMU should be sufficient for your needs. **They have wireless in all of the libraries, some classrooms, and some of the cafeterias**. The computer labs aren't usually filled. I think our facilities are on par with, or better, than the national average."

Q "Most dorms will have computers available for public use. **The network is a standard college network**. Initially, there are problems with people trying to connect. It is recommended to have a computer, especially in your freshman year because of the writing classes you are required to take. You will do a lot of writing your freshman year. There is a computer lab at the student center that is almost never full except lunchtime. It is pretty easy to get access all over campus."

Q "Definitely bring your own computer. We have computer labs, but **you will have to wait a while to use them**. Everyone here has a computer, and so should you."

Q "I have **never had a problem finding a computer to use**. They are everywhere. I suggest bringing your own if you like stuff like AIM. But for the purpose of schoolwork, it is not really necessary."

Q "Every student needs their own computer. I don't really go to the computer labs that much. **I do use SMU's high-speed network**, and it's been pretty good to me so far."

Q "You have got to have your own computer. **Just about all of the classes require using computers**, whether it's to download notes or to do research. It's a survival tool."

Q "I've only used the campus computers in the student center occasionally to check e-mail in the middle of the day or something. I've used the dorm ones when my printer had a fit. **I've never had a problem getting on a computer**. It would be nice if they had wireless campus-wide like a lot of other schools have now. Bringing a computer is just way easier, but I guess it's not necessary. I don't want to be anywhere else but my room when I'm doing homework, so if you're a procrastinator like me, get a computer. Rarely do people bring their computers to class. There are some, though."

Q "I have never had a problem getting on a computer at the library. There are also **tons of computer labs in the ME and EE buildings**. I would say that you definitely need to bring your own computer because most professors e-mail you assignments. It is really annoying and inconvenient to walk all the way to the library just to check your e-mail."

Q "**The computer network is not great**. It is only suitable for surfing the Internet. Anything else is either banned or not supported by the campus. It makes free time difficult to enjoy. You should bring your computer for sure, but expect to encounter some problems if you are not a casual user."

Q "Having a computer is convenient, but not necessary. I rarely take my laptop to the library. There are about eight libraries, most of which have computer labs. I study there and use those computers. As far as the network goes, it is fast and the tech department is pretty helpful. **We even have our own computer store**."

Q "The labs are not very crowded. **I lasted my freshman year without a computer, but it was a hassle** to walk to the labs to print the papers."

The College Prowler Take On...
Computers

Having a computer on campus is always a blessing, but it is mainly for those who would rather do schoolwork at home as opposed to walking to a library to face a time limit. When I was a freshman, I did not have a printer. The dorms feature computer outlets in every room as well as computers and printers in the main lobbies. I would type my paper in my room, save it on a disk, and travel downstairs to print it. The entire process was simplistic and painless.

I have only had to use the 24-hour computer lab in the student center a few times, and it has never been full. The only problem with those computers is that they do not allow you to save your Word documents or anything of that sort onto a disk. You either have to e-mail it to yourself or ask for assistance from the help desk. Those computers are primarily for checking e-mail and surfing the Internet. The computers in libraries are used more to do homework and research. Many students choose to write papers in those spots because something about the library forces them to focus. All of the computers on campus are up-to-date and are constantly being replaced with new ones. The only pain is printing. You must first buy a copy card, put money on it, and then proceed to print. What seems odd to me is that SMU is well-endowed but has poor computer facilities.

C+

The College Prowler® Grade on

Computers: C+

A high grade in Computers designates that computer labs are available, the computer network is easily accessible, and the campus' computing technology is up-to-date.

Facilities

The Lowdown On...
Facilities

Athletic Center:
The Cinco Center

Dedman Center for
Lifetime Sports

Student Center:
Hughes-Trigg Student Center

Libraries:
11

Campus Size:
170 acres

**Popular Places
to Chill:**
Hughes-Trigg Student Center

Outside residence halls

The pool

What Is There to Do?

SMU offers several activities to keep you from yawning. You can burn calories in the gym, get a quick meal, tan at the pool, watch a free movie showing in the student center, volunteer, audition for a production such as *Mustang Idol* or *The Vagina Monologues*, go see a theatre or dance production, critique a student art show, attend a concert, go to the on-site museum, join a club, attend a lecture series, or take a leisurely walk.

Movie Theater on Campus?

No. There are movie showings, but no actual theatre where students can go on any given day.

Bowling on Campus?

No

Bar on Campus?

No, SMU is a dry campus.

Coffeehouse on Campus?

No; there is a place to get specialty coffees, though.

Favorite Things to Do

Even though SMU is still trying to recover from its terrible fate in the '80s (the football team was sanctioned), students tailgate with full force anyway. With a new coach and a revamped program, SMU might just have a chance, which is why there are more students attending the games lately. During the day, most students enjoy a quick dip at the pool or just go to tan with their friends. Every semester, the dance department holds Brown Bag, where students can bring their lunch and watch an hour-long performance. There are featured events hosted by different organizations in the student center every day.

Students Speak Out On...
Facilities

> "The facilities on campus are adequate. They are not very elaborate, but they get the job done."

Q "The **athletic department facilities stink**. But they are renovating . . . like always . . . not to mention raising tuition for it . . . like always."

Q "The dorms vary. There are the yucky ones, nice ones, quiet ones, loud ones, fun ones, and cozy ones. The **computers vary by location**, but the best ones are in the libraries. The student center is nice . . . much like any other."

Q "**The facilities are very nice**, but I don't know if they are functional."

Q "As far as athletic facilities go, by the time you are through reading this book, the brand new workout facility will be erected with a brand new smoothie bar. As far as sports go, the **athletic facilities are exceptional**. The student center is very nice. They will always update and change it based on students' responses. The dining halls and eateries are changed every year according to surveys. The post office, computer lab, and the market are all in the student center."

Q "For the school that we go to, we should have a much nicer gym. The other facilities are pretty good, though. I am, on the other hand, getting bored of seeing **the same building being built over and over again**. Every time they build a new one, it looks just like all the other ones."

Q "The facilities on campus **are good and improve every year**. For example, millions of dollars are going into the construction of the new gym on campus that will be available to the entire student body."

Q "Well, if you're a business student, then **you have the best facilities money can buy**, and there are more great facilities on the way. If you are any other major, just be happy that you don't have to study outside because your buildings aren't ever getting repaired."

Q "Everything at SMU is **pretty top notch**."

Q "The **student center is kind of shabby** in my opinion. I just don't think it is very inviting for students. That is a big problem."

Q "I would like **something to be offered 24-hours a day** (especially a gym)."

Q "**Hughes-Trigg is convenient to get to**, and there are always people there hanging out. The Cinco Center is really tiny and cramped, but Dedman is being renovated."

Q "The newer facilities found in **the engineering buildings are up-to-date and enjoyable**. Computers outside of the engineering facilities are not that great, but you also do not need them that much. Some of the places seem a bit crowded and stuffy."

Q "The facilities are **top notch and getting better**. I've never seen so many new and refurbished buildings in one place."

Q "The pools are nice, and we are getting a newly renovated and expanded gym. **The student center is nice, because it is centrally located**. I rarely go there, though. We are constantly building and improving, a true sign of dedicated alumni and staff. The libraries look better and more equipped every year."

The College Prowler Take On...
Facilities

SMU has quite an advantage when it comes to generous donors; however, sometimes it is difficult to see where all of the money is being dispensed. Several students have complained about the facilities on campus and wonder why they are not better equipped or rebuilt yet. SMU is, on the other hand, in the process of adding the Dedman Lifetime Center for Sports, which features a 165,000-sq.-ft. expansion, along with a climbing wall, water park, 15,000-sq.-ft. weight room, new volleyball and basketball courts, new gym equipment, an outdoor adventure area with tents and kayak checkouts, a recreational pool, an expanded track, and much more. The new athletic center will be an immense improvement from its old structure. So not only will the new facility be a great place to hang out, but students will also be much more satisfied and inclined to work out.

Aside from the athletic center, the campus in general is gorgeous and worth bragging about. While it may seem as though the facilities are never improving, that is definitely not the case. Every year, SMU makes new plans to improve each and every school building as well as things like roads and parking garages. The plans are available online and so is their expected completion date. At first glance, one can see the green shrubbery and flowers all over campus, which is a plus because most of Texas's grass is yellow. The more you walk around this campus, the more you will see how nice the facilities look. Don't be dismayed if you see sidewalks and buildings being ripped apart—construction never ends here.

C

The College Prowler® Grade on

Facilities: C

A high Facilities grade indicates that the campus is aesthetically pleasing and well-maintained; facilities are state-of-the-art, and libraries are exceptional. Other determining factors include the quality of both athletic and student centers and an abundance of things to do on campus.

Campus Dining

The Lowdown On...
Campus Dining

Freshman Meal Plan Requirement?
Yes

Meal Plan Average Cost:
$3,600

Places to Grab a Bite with Your Meal Plan:

Chick-fil-A
Location: Hughes-Trigg

Food: American/chicken-based

Favorite Dish: Chicken sandwich

Hours: Monday–Thursday 8 a.m.–7 p.m., Friday 8 a.m.–5 p.m.

Java City Cyber Café

Location: Hughes-Trigg, Dedman Center

Food: Coffee, pastries

Favorite Dish: Mocha

Hours: (Hughes-Trigg) Monday–Friday 7:30 a.m.–12 a.m.
(Dedman Center) Monday–Friday 11:30 a.m.–8 p.m.

Mac's Place

Location: McElvaney Hall

Food: American

Favorite Dish: Cheeseburger and fries

Hours: Monday–Thursday 11 a.m.–2:15 p.m., and 4:30 p.m.–7:30 p.m., Friday 11 a.m.–2:15 p.m.

The Market

Location: Hughes-Trigg

Food: Grocery Store with Java Hut and Freshens

Favorite Dish: California rolls

Hours: Sunday 2 p.m.–6 p.m., Monday–Thursday 8 a.m.–8 p.m., Friday 8 a.m.–4:30 p.m., Saturday 10 a.m.–4 p.m.

Midnight Express

Location: McElvaney Hall

Food: Mini-grocery store

Favorite: Frozen pizza

Hours: Sunday–Thursday 8 p.m.–12 a.m.

Montague's Deli

Location: Hughes-Trigg

Food: Sandwiches/paninis

Favorite Dish: Chicken caesar sandwich

Hours: Monday–Friday 10:30 a.m.–2:30 p.m.

RFoC (Real Food on Campus)

Location: Umphrey Lee Center

Food: Various/buffet style and salad bar

Favorite Dish: Grilled sandwiches and nachos

Hours: Sunday 9:30 a.m.–11 p.m., Monday–Thursday 1 a.m.–11 p.m., Friday 7 a.m.–7 p.m., Saturday 9:30 a.m.–7 p.m.

SMUothies

Location: Dedman Center

Food: Smoothies, drinks

Favorite Dish: Raspberry smoothie

Hours: Monday–Friday 7:30 a.m.–10 p.m., Saturday 10 a.m.–10 p.m., Sunday 2 p.m.–10 p.m.

Snack Exchange

Location: Fincher Building

Food: Snacks, drinks

Favorite Dish: Chips and a soda

Hours: Monday–Thursday 10:30 a.m.–7 p.m., Friday 10:30 a.m.–6 p.m.

Subway

Location: Hughes-Trigg

Food: Sandwiches

Favorite Dish: Turkey breast combo

Hours: Monday–Thursday 10:30 a.m.–7 p.m., Friday 10:30 a.m.–6 p.m.

Other Options

SMU offers Pony Express dollars that can be added onto your SMU ID. That money can be used to eat at off-campus places, such as Jason's Deli, Jersey Mike's, Stromboli Café, Jimmy John's, Roly Poly, La Madeleine, and others. It functions as a pre-paid debit card and can be used at all SMU retail food centers.

Off-Campus Places to Use Your Meal Plan

None

24-Hour On-Campus Eating?

None

Did You Know?

Twice a year, **SMU Dining Services posts a customer survey online**. Just by completing it, you are automatically entered into a drawing for a prize. In the past, they have featured a round-trip American Airlines ticket to anywhere in the country.

Campus Dining

"The dining halls are good at first, but they get old really quickly. Really quickly. The breakfast at Umph [Umphrey Lee Center] is the best. Besides that, Subway and Chick-fil-A are okay, depending on your mood."

Q "**Dining halls get old fast**. They should be 24-hours. The best place to eat on campus is Chick-fil-A."

Q "The food on campus is really good. Breakfast is outstanding because **you can get made-to-order omelets and anything you want, really**. The success of our on-campus kitchens is based on variety in the everyday menu and constantly making new things. Other than the cafeterias, we have a Chick-fil-A, a Subway, a coffee shop and some other small food stations."

Q "**Bad**!"

Q "**The dining hall food is exceptional**. The only problem with them is that they're serving almost the same food for the entire semester. No matter what quality food you're eating, it will get old after a while. The student center has a few popular fast food restaurants if you're getting tired of eating eggs benedict. It's not the sterile, white-tile, white-wall, garish halogen lights standard cafeteria. The school has gone to great lengths to make it visibly pleasing and comfortable. Sometimes they even have musicians perform there."

Q "**Dining halls are dining halls**. Other food around campus is decent. La Madeleine, Roly Poly, Stromboli Cafe, and Jimmy John's are all within walking distance."

Q "I never really liked Mac's Place. It was cool when you were a freshman because everyone hung out there. **Umphrey Lee is pretty good**. They have a nicer selection than Mac's Place. They have way more hot meal selections and are open later. The places to eat in the student center are convenient. There's a little something for everyone."

Q "In the student center, the food is great. **There is a Subway, a Chick-fil-A, and another sandwich place**. The cafeterias are okay. I mean, what can you really expect from a cafeteria anyway?"

Q "**Food on campus is mediocre**. The cafeteria is great during lunch hours. The best place to eat is Chick-fil-A, which is located in the Varsity."

Q "Umphrey Lee is all right. **It doesn't have the best food**, but it has food nonetheless."

Q "Dining on campus is all right. **It's not bad and it's not good**. If you alternate between Mac's Place and Umphrey Lee, a week on, a week off, you will be fine. Some of the selections in Hughes-Trigg are okay."

Q "**It is the greatest for the first two weeks**. After that, bring on Mane Street."

Q "The food is all right. It's nothing special. **The hours are not that great**, especially for college students. The dining halls are nice and are always clean. One of them has a baby grand piano. Really, I wish there was something 24-hours where you could hang out and get a meal. There's food to walk to off campus that accepts the student card, which is a bonus."

Q "Dining halls are as expected, nothing spectacular, similar routines in food. However, there have been improvements—some in quality but mainly in aesthetics. There are some places to eat in the student center. **Better food can be found off campus**, anywhere from two minutes to ten minutes away, where you can satisfy any craving. Places to check out: Freebirds and New York Subs."

The College Prowler Take On...
Campus Dining

Almost every student will admit that the dining on campus is great . . . until their breaking point surfaces and they wish they were still eating mom's homemade pot roast. Some are forced to commit to a semester of Ramen. Everything can become a bit tiresome over time, especially if it is repetitive and over exhausted. All resident students must buy a meal plan. Each plan is the same price, but it differs based on the number of "Flex Dollars" chosen. Flex Dollars can be used anywhere with a cash register operated by SMU Dining Services. There are two other flexible meal plans offered for seniors or graduate students, both of which are less expensive. Most students, even upperclassmen, rave about Umphrey Lee's lunch selections. This cafeteria features a large salad bar, Asian cuisine, American hamburgers and fries, a homestyle section, a grilled sandwich and wrap section, and many others. Umphrey Lee's choices change every day. With the addition of Subway, more students are eating on campus during the lunchtime hour. SMU also offers other options. The school is conveniently located next to Hillcrest Avenue and Mockingbird. Both streets offer more dining options, and most of them accept Pony Express.

SMU Dining Services conducts a survey every semester to see what students like and dislike, as well as what they would like to add (hence the addition of Subway). The idea of eating on campus has an unpleasant stigma attached to it; however, having someone else clean your dishes and cook several different types of food is the upside of having a meal plan.

C+

The College Prowler® Grade on Campus Dining: C+

Our grade on Campus Dining addresses the quality of both school-owned dining halls and independent on-campus restaurants as well as the price, availability, and variety of food.

Off-Campus Dining

The Lowdown On...
Off-Campus Dining

Restaurant Prowler:
Popular Places to Eat!

Blue Fish

Food: Japanese

3519 Greenville Avenue, Lower Greenville

(214) 824-3474

Fax: (214) 823-2890

Cool Features: Volcano rolls, crab meat sushi.

Price: $15–$20 per person

(Blue Fish, continued)

Hours: Monday–Sunday 11:30 a.m.–2 p.m., 5 p.m.–10:30 p.m.

Buca di Beppo

Food: Southern Italian

7843 Park Lane, Northwest Dallas

(214) 361-8462

Fax: (214) 739-4734

Cool Features: Small and large portions designed for two people or a family.

Price: $15–$20 per person

→

(Buca di Beppo, continued)

Hours: Monday–Thursday
5 p.m.–10 p.m., Friday
5 p.m.–11 p.m., Saturday
12 p.m.–11 p.m., Sunday
12 p.m.–9 p.m.

Café Brazil

Food: Brazilian,
Latin American

6420 N. Central
Expressway, Park Cities

(214) 691-7791

www.cafebrazil.com

Cool Features: Breakfast,
lunch, and dinner served at
all times, rosemary potatoes,
chicken crepes, several types
of Brazilian coffee.

Price: $10 and under

Hours: Daily 24 hours

Campisi's Egyptian Restaurant

Food: Italian

5665 E. Mockingbird Lane,
Park Cities

(214) 827-0355

Cool Features: Local favorite,
two dining areas.

Price: $10 and under

Hours: Sunday–Thursday
11 a.m.–10 p.m., Friday–
Saturday 11 a.m.–11 p.m.

The Cheesecake Factory

Food: Various

7700 W. Northwest Highway,
Northwest Dallas

(214) 373-4844

Cool Features: 35
different cheesecakes.

Price: $15–$20 per person

Hours: Monday–Thursday
11 a.m.–11 p.m., Friday–
Saturday 11 a.m.–12:30 a.m.,
Sunday 10:30 a.m.–11 p.m.

Chipotle

Food: Burritos and tacos

7700 N. Central Expressway,
Dallas

(469) 232-0963

Fax: (469) 232-0950

Cool Features: Giant burritos.

Price: $7–$10 per person

Hours: Daily 11 a.m.–10 p.m.

Chuy's

Food: Mexican

4544 McKinney Avenue,
Knox Henderson

(214) 559-2489

Cool Features: Chuy's
special, sopapillas and honey,
chile con queso.

Price: $8–$10 per person

Hours: Sunday–Thursday
11 a.m.–10 p.m., Friday–
Saturday 11 a.m.–11 p.m.

Cuba Libre Café

Food: Caribbean, Latin American, South American

2822 N. Henderson Avenue, Knox Henderson

(214) 827-2820

Fax: (214) 827-2189

Cool Features: Two levels, outdoor patios.

Price: $16–$20 per person

Hours: Sunday–Wednesday 11 a.m.–12 a.m. Thursday–Saturday 11 a.m.–1 a.m.

Freebirds World Burrito

Food: Burritos, Mexican

5500 Greenville Avenue, Suite 209

(214) 265-9992

Fax: (214) 265-9997

Cool Features: Four sizes of burritos, Freebirds BBQ sauce.

Price: $10 and under per person

Hours: Monday–Thursday 11 a.m.–10:30 p.m., Friday–Sunday 11 a.m.–11 p.m.

Houston's Restaurant

Food: American and Caribbean

8300 Preston Road, Suite A, Park Cities

(214) 691-8991

Fax: (214) 691-8452

(Houston's, continued)

Cool Features: Spinach and artichoke dip, Hawaiian marinated steak.

Price: $20–$25 per person

Hours: Monday–Thursday 11 a.m.–10:30 p.m., Friday–Saturday 11:00 a.m.–11:30 p.m., Sunday 10:30 a.m.–10:30 p.m.

Jersey Mike's

Food: Subs

5521 Greenville Avenue, Suite 108B & 109

(214) 692-6981

www.jerseymikes.com

Cool Features: Mike's Way, chicken Philly, Jersey Mike's super sub.

Price: $8 and under

Hours: Monday–Saturday 10 a.m.–9 p.m., Sunday 11 a.m.–8 p.m.

The Mansion on Turtle Creek

Food: Southwestern

2821 Turtle Creek Boulevard, Dallas

(214) 559-2100

www.mansiononturtlecreek.com

Cool Features: Rated as a top restaurant by *Travel & Leisure*, elegant dining.

(The Mansion, continued)

Price: $25–$50 per person

Hours: Lunch, Monday–Saturday 11:30 a.m.–2 p.m.; Dinner, Sunday–Wednesday 6 p.m.–10 p.m., Thursday–Saturday 6 p.m.–10:30 p.m.; Brunch, Sunday 11 a.m.–2 p.m.

Mi Cocina

Food: Mexican

77 Highland Park Village, Highland Park

(214) 521-6426

Cool Features: Mico's #4 tacos al carbon, Mama's chicken, fajitas

Price: $15 and under

Hours: Daily 11 a.m.–10 p.m.

Pei Wei Asian Diner

Food: Asian

3001 Knox Street, Knox Park

(214) 219-0000

Fax: (214) 522-2970

Cool Features: Minced chicken in cool lettuce wraps, Dan Dan noodle bowl, Mandarin kung pao.

Price: $10 and under

Hours: Daily 11:30 a.m.–10 p.m.

P.F. Chang's

Food: Chinese

225 Northpark Center, Dallas

(214) 265-8669

www.pfchangs.com

Cool Features: Great wine list, traditional Chinese dishes and creative new dishes.

Price: $9–$14 per person

Hours: Sunday–Thursday 11 a.m.–11 p.m, Friday–Saturday 11 a.m.–12 a.m.

Pluckers Wing Bar

Food: Wings

5505 Greenville Avenue, Suite 406, Dallas

(214) 363-WING

www.pluckers.net

Cool Features: Wing Nut Club for frequent customers, Hall of Flame.

Price: $7–$14 per person

Hours: Sunday–Wednesday 11 a.m.–2 a.m, Thursday–Saturday 11 a.m.–3 a.m.

Rockfish

Food: Seafood

5331 East Mockingbird Lane #160,Park Cities

(214) 823-8444

www.rockfishseafood.com

(Rockfish, continued)

Cool Features: Santa Fe fish tacos, Alberto's seafood enchiladas, Po Boy sandwiches, Rock-A-Rita.

Price: $10–$15 per person

Hours: Monday–Thursday 11 a.m.–10 p.m., Friday–Saturday 11 a.m.–11 p.m., Sunday 11 a.m.–9 p.m.

Sevy's

Food: American

8201 Preston Rd., Dallas

(214) 265-7389

Cool Features: Private dining, outdoor patios, putting green.

Price: $15–$25 per person

Hours: Monday–Thursday 11 a.m.–10 p.m., Friday 11 a.m.–11 p.m., Saturday 11 a.m.–2:30 p.m., 5 p.m.–11 p.m., Sunday 5 p.m.–9 p.m.

Simply Fondue

Food: Fondue

2108 Greenville Avenue, Lower Greenville

(214) 827-8878

Cool Features: Four course dinner (nine different types of chocolate fondue for dessert) for two or more.

Price: $30–$40 per person

Hours: Sunday–Thursday 6 p.m.–10 p.m., Friday 6 p.m.–12:00 a.m., Saturday 5 p.m.–12:00 a.m.

Snuffer's

Food: American

3526 Greenville Avenue, Lower Greenville

(214) 826-6850

Cool Features: Cheddar fries, Snuffer's cheeseburger.

Price: $5–$10 per person

Hours: Sunday–Thursday 11 a.m.–12 a.m., Friday–Saturday 11 a.m.–2 a.m.

Student Favorites:

Chipotle

Houston's Restaurant

Mi Cocina

Pei Wei

Late-Night Food:

Café Brazil

Cuba Libre Café

Snuffer's

24-Hour Eating:

Café Brazil

Closest Grocery Stores:

Tom Thumb

7000 Snider Plaza,
Park Cities

(214) 346-9371

Kroger

5665 E. Mockingbird Lane,
Park Cities

(214) 826-2967

Central Market

5750 E. Lovers Lane,
Park Cities

(214) 234-7000

Whole Foods Market

2218 Lower Greenville
Avenue

(214) 824-1744

Best Pizza:

Campisi's Egyptian Restaurant

Best Chinese:

Pei Wei Asian Diner

Best Breakfast:

Café Brazil

The Cheesecake Factory

Best Wings:

Plucker's

Best Healthy:

Central Market

Whole Foods

Best Place to Take Your Parents:

Blue Fish

Cuba Libre

Houston's Restaurant

Rockfish

Other Places to Check Out:

Abacus	Magarita Ranch
Blue Goose	Nick & Sam's
Blue Mesa Grill	Penne Pomodoro
Bob's Steak & Chop House	Potbelly Sandwich Works
Café Express	Stromboli Café
California Pizza Kitchen	Taj Mahal Indian Restaurant
EatZi's	Three Forks
Fogo De Chao	Whataburger

Did You Know?

The **frozen margarita** was invented in Dallas.

Dallasites consume the **most picante sauce** in the nation.

The **chicken fajita** was invented in Dallas.

Dallas is home to more restaurants per person than the Big Apple. This includes more than **7,000 restaurants**.

Students Speak Out On...
Off-Campus Dining

{ **"You've got every kind of food you could want within just a few miles of campus. That's the advantage of being in a metropolitan area."**

Q "It all **depends on how much and how far you want to go**. Nothing is really close besides pizza or small spots in Snider Plaza. I like anything in Highland Park Village. EatZi's, Central Market, and the Mansion on Turtle Creek are all really good, if you want to sell your first born—but it may be worth it."

Q "There are **tons of really yummy places to eat**, and they are all very close. I like Snuffer's, Chipotle, Margarita Ranch, and Café Express."

Q "**Dining off campus is decent**. The best Indian restaurant is the Taj Mahal."

Q "**Every restaurant there is can be found within ten minutes of campus** since we're right in the heart of a major city. It's not hard to find good places to eat. I love Freebirds, Sevy's, California Pizza Kitchen, Jersey Mike's, and Pei Wei."

Q "Dining off campus is great. Dallas has a metric ton of great places to eat, and **some of them don't cost you an arm and a leg**."

Q "The food in Dallas, especially around campus, is great. **There are so many places to choose from**. I like P.F. Chang's, Penne Pomodoro, and many others."

Q "The main place I often go to is Chipotle. **Good food at a great price**."

Q "There are many excellent cheap restaurants within walking distance from residence halls. There are even more, both inexpensive and expensive, within a five-mile radius of campus. The ones you can walk to are great, and the ones you can drive to are even better. The Park Cities caters to the young, hip crowd. Hillcrest is a great street, where most of the restaurants are laid out in a strip-mall style facing the campus. **There is a small quaint little shopping center called Snider Plaza with over 30 store fronts**. Knox Park features Pei Wei and Potbelly Sandwich Works. Greenville Avenue has almost every fast food restaurant you'll ever eat at . . . except Big Boy and Hardees. So if you like Hardees, you shouldn't come to Texas. If you're not from Texas, you're missing out on the best fast food restaurant: Whataburger. You should come to school just for Whataburger. It's also open 24 hours a day and serves breakfast from 11 a.m. to 11 p.m. Central Market is the premium grocery store in the area. If you don't want to go out to eat, you can pick up something there and heat it up at home. The Mansion on Turtle Creek is the coup de gras of Dallas dining. For special occasions or the high roller, it is the best restaurant in North Dallas. Sevy's, P.F. Chang's, the Cheesecake Factory, and Blue Mesa are also great."

Q "There are many restaurants and places to shop anywhere you would want to go in Dallas. **The list is too long**."

Q "You must eat at **Snuffer's, Stromboli Café, Plucker's, and Jersey Mike's**."

Q "I mainly eat at Snuffer's a lot. **I can't really afford off-campus meals, except the 99 cents menu**, but that's the nice thing about Dallas. It can feed me!"

Q "**Food off campus is much better than on campus**. The Dallas area has many types of food to try and many good restaurants. Two that are a must see: Abacus and Fogo De Chao."

Q "I love to eat lunch at Central Market, because it has everything, and you can get exactly what you want. **Blue Goose is my true pride**. I eat there once a week. It is the best 'Tex Mex' in Dallas. I love Pei Wei, too, because we don't have that in San Diego."

The College Prowler Take On...
Off-Campus Dining

Gaining the Freshman 15 is an overall fear for all college students. Instead of 15 pounds, it is more likely to be 30 or 40, simply because all of the food off campus is more delectable. Every student has difficulty choosing one particular favorite place to eat. It is much simpler to choose one favorite per genre. Because SMU is located in a posh and hip area, dining off campus can definitely become a bit pricey. Luckily, there are places like Snuffer's, Café Brazil, Chipotle, Chuy's, Campisi's, and several others to balance out the more expensive places. Many students have dined at the Mansion at least once (mainly with their parents or credit card), as well as Nick and Sam's, Three Forks, or Bob's Chop House (for excellent steak).

Dallas is known to have the best shopping in the country. Normally, if a city features superb shopping, it also showcases dining. Dallas happens to be the home of the best restaurants in the nation. Every type of food can be found here in the heart of Texas. Due to its location, Dallas features exquisite and authentic Mexican cuisine, as well as delicious Tex Mex. Most students eat Mexican at least once a week because of this phenomenon. The possibilities are endless. If there is any hesitation as to where to dine, it will be spurred by an overwhelming list of restaurants. It is easy to become accustomed to a certain taste and specific restaurant, but if you are ever feeling adventurous, Dallas is an immense city to explore.

A

The College Prowler® Grade on

Off-Campus
Dining: A

A high Off-Campus Dining grade implies that off-campus restaurants are affordable, accessible, and worth visiting. Other factors include the variety of cuisine and the availability of alternative options (vegetarian, vegan, Kosher, etc.).

Campus Housing

The Lowdown On...
Campus Housing

Undergrads Living On Campus:
40%

Room Types:
Singles, double, triples; with community, suite, or private bathroom units

Best Dorms:
Cockrell-McIntosh
McElvaney
Morrison-McGinnis
Virginia-Snider

Worst Dorms:
Mary Hay
Perkins
Peyton
Shuttles
Smith

Number of Dormitories:
11

Number of University-Owned Apartments:
557 apartments

Dormitories:

Boaz Hall
Community: First-year
Floors: Four plus basement
Total Occupancy: 242
Bathrooms: Community
Coed: Yes
Residents: Freshmen
Room Types: Double, triple
Special Features: Lounges and microwaves on every floor, computer room, built-in furniture, elevator

Cockrell-McIntosh Hall
Community: Four-class
Floors: Four plus basement
Total Occupancy: 209
Bathrooms: Suite
Coed: Yes
Residents: Freshmen, sophomores, juniors, seniors
Room Types: Single, double
Special Features: Study/ computer room in the suite, movable furniture, cable TV in each room, elevator

Daniel House
Community: Transfer and upper classmen
Floors: Two story townhouse-style apartments
Total Occupancy: 39
Bathrooms: Private
Coed: Yes

(Daniel House, continued)
Residents: Sophomores, juniors, seniors
Room Types: Three single bedrooms per townhouse
Special Features: Furnished, water and electric included, courtyard area

Hawk Hall
Community: Family-style one-bedroom apartments
Floors: Three
Total Occupancy: 34 apartments
Bathrooms: Private
Coed: Yes
Residents: Freshmen, sophomores, juniors, seniors
Room Types: Apartment
Special Features: Kitchenette, furnished, sink in the room

Martin Hall
Community: Single and married graduate student efficiency apartments
Floors: Three
Total Occupancy: 42 apartments
Bathrooms: Private
Coed: Yes
Residents: Freshmen, sophomores, juniors, seniors
Room Types: Apartment
Special Features: Kitchenette, furnished, sink in the room

Mary Hay Hall

Community: Fine arts

Floors: Four plus basement

Total Occupancy: 136

Bathrooms: Suite

Coed: Yes

Residents: Freshmen, sophomores, juniors, seniors

Room Types: Single, double

Special Features: Art gallery, painting studio, dance performance space, built-in furniture, elevator

McElvaney Hall

Community: First-year

Floors: Four plus basement

Total Occupancy: 260

Bathrooms: Community

Coed: Yes

Residents: Freshmen

Room Types: Double

Special Features: Each floor has a lounge with computers, area desk on first floor, Mac's Place and Midnight Express on first floor, cable TV in every room, movable furniture, elevator

Moore Hall

Community: Upperclass and graduate efficiency apartments

Floors: Four

Total Occupancy: 120

Bathrooms: Private

Coed: Yes

(Moore Hall, continued)

Residents: Sophomores, juniors, seniors

Room Types: Double, apartment

Special Features: Kitchenette, furnished, cable TV in every apartment, elevator, sink in the room

Morrison-McGinnis Hall

Community: Four-class

Floors: Four plus basement

Total Occupancy: 201

Bathrooms: Community, suite

Coed: Yes

Residents: Freshmen, sophomores, juniors, seniors

Room Types: Single, double

Special Features: Lounge on every floor, study/computer rooms in the suite, movable furniture, elevator, cable TV in each room

Multicultural House

Community: Unity and diversity

Floors: Two

Total Occupancy: 14

Bathrooms: Community

Coed: Yes

Residents: Sophomores, juniors, seniors

Room Types: Double

Special Features: Large community kitchen, movable furniture

Perkins Hall

Community: Hilltop Scholars; first-year

Floors: Three

Total Occupancy: 85

Bathrooms: Community

Coed: Yes

Residents: Freshmen

Room Types: Single, double

Special Features: Kitchens on every floor, movable furniture, laundry facilities on two floors, high ceilings, classes in the residence hall

Peyton Hall

Community: Fine arts

Floors: Three

Total Occupancy: 102

Bathrooms: Suite

Coed: Yes

Residents: Freshmen, sophomores, juniors, seniors

Room Types: Double

Special Features: Largest rooms of all halls, laundry facilities on two floors, elevator, movable furniture

Service House

Community: Community service

Floors: 2

Total Occupancy: 28

Bathrooms: Suite

Coed: Yes

Residents: Sophomores, juniors, seniors

(Service House, continued)

Room Types: Double

Special Features: House pool table, ping pong table, large community kitchen, movable furniture

Shuttles Hall

Community: Four-class

Floors: Four plus basement

Total Occupancy: 192

Bathrooms: Suite

Coed: Yes

Residents: Freshmen, sophomores, juniors, seniors

Room Types: Double

Special Features: Microwaves available on three floors, hall pool table, built-in furniture, elevator

Smith Hall

Community: Wellness Connection

Floors: Three

Total Occupancy: 85

Bathrooms: Community

Coed: Yes

Residents: Freshmen, sophomores, juniors, seniors

Room Types: Single, double

Special Features: Hall pool table, kitchens on two floors, movable furniture

→

SMU Apartments

Community: Upperclassmen

Floors: Two

Total Occupancy: 240 (individual apartments)

Bathrooms: Private

Coed: Yes

Residents: Sophomores, juniors, seniors

Room Types: One-bedroom, two-bedroom, effieciencies

Special Features: The building is owned and run by SMU, but residents pay monthly rent.

Virginia-Snider Hall

Community: Honors

Floors: 4

Total Occupancy: 258

Bathrooms: Community, suite

Coed: Yes

Residents: Freshmen, sophomores, juniors, seniors

Room Types: Single, double, triple

Special Features: Sink in the room (Virginia), study room in the suite, cable TV in each room, movable furniture, two elevators, study lounges, two laundry facilities

Bed Type

Twin extra-long (75"–80" long), some bunk and loft beds

Available for Rent

Mini-refrigerator

Cleaning Service?

Community bathrooms and lounges are cleaned daily. Suite bathrooms are cleaned once a week.

You Get

Bed, desk, bookshelf, dresser, closet, Ethernet connection, telephone with local service and voicemail

Also Available

Substance-free residence hall, diversity hall, community service hall, Shared Interest Communities

Did You Know?

About **2,000 students** live in one of the eleven residence halls.

Residence Life & Student Housing (RLSH) offers several **intramural sports** and other activities for residents to participate in.

A few dorms feature **Learning Enhancement Assistants** whose primary job is to monitor first-year students' academic progress and be a connection to the Learning Enhancement Center, which is a free tutoring service.

Residents on campus have three different types of bathrooms in the dorms:

Community – Students share a large bathroom facility (one female and one male facility per floor). These are typically located in first-year residence halls.

Suite – Students share a semi-private bathroom with no more than four students.

Private – Students share a single bathroom (mainly between no more than two students).

Students Speak Out On...
Campus Housing

"Perkins is great. It is an older dorm, but those dorms have a fun and homey feel. Boaz is crazy, but good for people who stay up until 4 a.m. every day."

Q "There's a party, boring, rich girl, and random dorm. The rich and crazy kids live in Boaz. Avoid Boaz. The more serious student lives in Cockrell-McIntosh. McElvaney houses mainly daddy's girls and pretty boys. Shuttles has the nice down-to-earth people."

Q "Anything in the South Quad is nice, but **very sterile and quiet**. Mary Hay is outgoing and great for theatrical people."

Q "Morrison-McGinnis is really great! **Avoid Mary Hay**."

Q "**The dorms are a lot of fun**. A lot of the dorms have been completely renovated with new walls, ceilings, carpet, and 90 channels of cable. For freshmen, the best dorms are McElvaney, Morrison-McGinnis, Cockrell-McIntosh—basically the South Quad. Boaz Hall is known as the party/freshman crazy dorm, which a lot of students will have fun in, but the problem is that it hasn't been renovated in a long time. The walls are very thin, and it's a difficult place to study. It's fun to go hang out there, but do not live there. Most of the North Quad dorms have been renovated. Peyton Hall has the largest rooms on campus. Hilltop Scholars even have their English classes right there in their dorm."

Q "It completely **depends on what sort of environment you want to live in**. Boaz is typically known as more of a party dorm. Mary Hay and Peyton are artsy. Virginia-Snider has the Honors kids. The South Quad usually has a good percentage of upperclassmen living in the non-freshmen dorms, since they are renovated."

Q "The dorms here, compared to other schools, are better. None of the dorms here have more than four levels. **Boaz is horrible, and if you're looking for accommodations, look elsewhere**. Peyton is nice if you want big rooms. The whole South Quad is a great place for freshmen. You'll get to know a lot of people, since that is mainly a freshman area."

Q "All the dorms in the South Quad are great and have been renovated. **The dorms in the North Quad, however, have not been renovated**. I'd stay away from living in the North Quad, unless you can get into Virginia-Snider."

Q "The dorms are good. **Peyton needs renovation**."

Q "**All the dorms are unique**. If you want a nice dorm, live in McElvaney, Morrison-McGinnis, or Virginia-Snider. If you want character, live in Mary Hay, Peyton, or Boaz."

Q "**Avoid Boaz and Shuttles**. They aren't that great. The best looking dorms are the ones you have to pay more for. Dorms like Perkins are good because they are so small and you get to know everyone."

Q "The dorms are nothing special. As a freshman, **I would suggest that you live in an all-freshmen dorm**! I loved Boaz because it was the typical college dorm. I met so many people. It's loud, so it may not be for everyone. It's definitely fun, and you make lots of friends."

Q "The dorms in general are **superior to most colleges**. The dorms that are nice are the Honors dorms (Virginia-Snider) and Cockrell-McIntosh. The dorms to avoid are Shuttles and Boaz. Most have cable TV, carpet, and are livable in size."

Q "Each dorm is different. There are two all-freshmen dorms, Boaz and McElvaney. Boaz tends to be a lot of fun, and there's always something happening. Cockrell-McIntosh and Morrison-McGinnis are really nice four-year dorms with cable. Virginia-Snider is the Honors dorm. Mary Hay and Peyton are the fine arts dorms. **There are some substance-free dorms as well**."

Q "When living in the dorms, **your experience all depends on which dorm you're in**. The dorms in the South Quad are all nice, but they are more expensive. The North Quad dorms are older, and that's where all of the art students live. I'd steer clear of Boaz if you're a first-year. You won't get much done with everyone sowing their wild oats around you."

Q "Every dorm has its own experience. Some say that you should stay away from Boaz (the party dorm), but I had a great experience. **You meet many people and make friends**. But after a while, you want some peace and quiet, and you move to better dorms like Cockrell-McIntosh."

Q "As an incoming freshman, I would choose an all-freshmen dorm, such as McElvaney. It is the nicer of the two. I lived in Peyton, which was quiet and spacious. The truth is, however, **you are going to have a blast no matter where you live**. The old dorms are fun to laugh at, and the new ones are cleaner."

The College Prowler Take On...
Campus Housing

It is required by the school that all first-year students live in the dorms. Even though some students choose to complain about their living situations, many will agree that the experience was worthwhile and essential to their introduction to SMU. The central areas in each quad provide a meeting spot and leisure area for the students. Many take advantage of the benches and beautiful landscaping SMU offers right in the middle of each quad. The only downside to living on campus is that some of the residence halls have not been renovated in a while. Peyton, Mary Hay, Shuttles, Perkins, Boaz, and Smith do not provide cable TV. The carpets in those dorms are decrepit, and the physical atmosphere in general has a somewhat retro feel. All of the halls are located in the same quad as a dining hall and require no more than five minutes to walk to class.

The dorms here at SMU function like a cabin at camp. Each student is supplied with the basics. The dorm rooms may not be spacious penthouse digs; however, the overall experience is the real focus. Everything can be enhanced, so think twice before complaining about your living situation. The beds can be bunked, pushed together, or lofted. If you find yourself uncomfortable in your bed, purchase a feather mattress cover. If you are tired of staring at white walls, then decorate them. The residence halls can be a fun experience if you are willing to let them provide everything that they are designed to, such as intramural sports, pizza and movie nights, game show nights, and much more.

B

The College Prowler® Grade on

Campus Housing: B

A high Campus Housing grade indicates that dorms are clean, well-maintained, and spacious. Other determining factors include variety of dorms, proximity to classes, and social atmosphere.

Off-Campus Housing

The Lowdown On...
Off-Campus Housing

Undergrads Living Off Campus:

60%

Best Time to Look for a Place:

Middle of second semester

Popular Complexes:

The Carlyle, the Gables, the Lofts at Mockingbird Station, the Phoenix, the Remington Signature Point

Average Rent For:

Studio Apt.: $700/month

1BR Apt.: $800/month

2BR Apt.: $1,300/month

For Assistance Contact:

Residence Life & Student Housing

www.smu.edu/housing

(214) 768-2407

E-mail: housing@smu.edu

Students Speak Out On...
Off-Campus Housing

> "If you have a car, it is worth it. However, at the same time, you don't get the college experience, and you don't meet anyone really new."

Q "It's great because you learn responsibility, but you can no longer just walk to class."

Q "There are a lot of places to live off campus. Being a well-established college city, the Park Cities offers a lot of apartments in a very broad price range. I have lived on campus all three years because I like being able to walk to class instead of trying to find parking. There are also on-campus apartments that are nice and convenient. Privacy and freedom can be expensive."

Q "On-campus apartments are nice for sophomore or junior year. For your senior year, go all out and have fun with your apartment."

Q "If you have a car, I'd say off-campus housing should be no problem. There are also a lot of on-campus apartments that are near classroom buildings and generally kept quite nice."

Q "It's not hard to find an apartment off campus. There are so many that are no more than two minutes away. It is worth it, especially because you don't have to share your room and you can get away from school life."

Q "On-campus apartments are the best bet. Everything in this area is really expensive."

Q "There are lots of places around campus to live after freshman year. However, **some can be pretty pricey**, and finding parking can be a real pain sometimes."

Q "Housing off campus is **hard without a car**, but it teaches you how to be independent and closer to the real world. In the long-run, it is worth it."

Q "Housing is very convenient, but **prices are relatively high compared to most university areas**. Living off campus is definitely worth it, but sometimes you can feel disconnected."

Q "You can do it, but **start looking early** to find a nice semi-affordable place that you can walk to, otherwise a car or bike is necessary. If you think you want an apartment, get a campus apartment, since it's affordable and walkable—I wouldn't go back to a dorm."

Q "My sophomore year, I lived in the sorority house, but for junior year, it was really easy to find an on-campus apartment. I think it is worth it, because **it's really close to campus** and you get your own privacy."

Q "I think it's not worth it, because **you lose on the college experience of meeting new people** and the ease of rolling out of bed and walking to class. It is not too difficult to find an apartment or town house off campus, and it's practically the same cost. But the downside is that you have to either walk farther or drive to campus."

Q "I live in the sorority house, which is technically off campus but very close. I love living there, because I can walk to class. **I would enjoy the privacy of living off campus**, but I do not have a car. Buying furniture in a place that I do not plan to settle in seems like a waste."

Q "Housing off campus is **really expensive in the general vicinity of school**, but there are a lot of places that aren't too far, if you are willing to drive a little more. Your best bet is to find a roommate to split the rent with."

Q "I really like off-campus housing because you can still be close to everything. You have your own room and living room. **It's nice because there's more freedom with the convenience of location**."

Q "I don't like the on-campus apartments. **They are not that much cheaper than living off campus**. At the Phoenix, if I want something fixed, I can call someone, and they come within an hour. They also exterminate once a week, too."

The College Prowler Take On...
Off-Campus Housing

Dallas has a vast selection of areas and complexes to live in, as well as a vast selection of price ranges. A large number of students choose to live off campus their sophomore through senior years, and their parents purchase condos or apartments for them. Living off campus has several benefits: freedom from RAs and rules, privacy, a real place to call 'home,' and not having to answer to school officials in general. When the time comes to start looking for housing, students do not have to arduously look around Dallas. Most students consistently pick the same complexes every year, and many of them are located here in the Park Cities. There are townhouses, houses, and apartment complexes on every corner and side of the campus, all of which are reasonably priced and comfortable. Once you venture out onto the expressway towards the Downtown, Knox-Henderson, and McKinney areas, the price range skyrockets. Because Dallas is such an urban and chic city, the cost of living is a bit higher, especially around areas of high traffic and business. However, since SMU is located in a college-friendly atmosphere, affordable housing is not difficult to track down.

Many students that live nearby can still walk to class. On the other hand, the farther you go, the earlier you will have to wake up to drive to class and park. Parking is a hassle at this school, so you will have to wake up maybe an hour or so before your class time just to secure a spot on the top level of the garage. If you enjoy rolling out of bed 10 or 15 minutes before class, living off campus is not for you. Another bonus of living off campus is that other SMU students will most likely live around you, too.

B+

The College Prowler® Grade on Off-Campus Housing: B+

A high grade in Off-Campus Housing indicates that apartments are of high quality, close to campus, affordable, and easy to secure.

Diversity

The Lowdown On...
Diversity

Native American:
1%

White:
75%

Asian American:
6%

International:
4%

African American:
5%

Out-of-State:
31%

Hispanic:
9%

Political Activity

Most of the students are conservative in nature as well as political views and background. There are many liberals—however, conservatives outnumber them. Although organizations, such as SMU Democrats, College Republicans, and Green Party, exist, no other political action occurs on this campus. People speak openly about their views, but just not very often.

Gay Pride

The student body in general is mildly accepting of SMU's small gay population. The gay community is widely accepted in the Meadows School of the Arts. Acceptance has yet to be fully incorporated by the rest of the campus.

Economic Status

Most SMU students come from upper- and upper-middle-class economic backgrounds.

Minority Clubs

The multicultural organizations on campus are somewhat recognizable, but they do not receive the same amount of attention as Greek Life or Christian groups. There are sixteen multicultural organizations, such as the Asian Council, College Hispanic American Students, Turkish Student Association, and the Association of Black Students. Each group sponsors activities in the student center.

Most Popular Religions

At a Methodist-affiliated school, the majority of students identify with the Methodist religion. There is also a large number of Catholic and Protestant students.

Students Speak Out On...
Diversity

> **"This campus is not diverse at all. It seems like you're always looking at the same people."**

Q "SMU is kind of diverse. There are many different nationalities. **The school is not into celebrating anything within nationalities**. Some races seem to segregate themselves from the rest of the population, but in the end, we are all equal, and most everyone respects the diversity."

Q "It's very diverse, but I think the school and student organizations have screwed themselves over for total integration. They encourage people of their respective race, such as Asian Council, and **discourage students from mixing some of the times**. Many times, you will have people of the same race hanging out with their same race. In a friendly way, the students have inadvertently done this. Greeks hang out with Greeks. Minorities with minorities. There's no tension or discord between the groups, but this has come to pass."

Q "This school is the **least diverse of all schools I've ever seen**."

Q "You can be an ostrich, stick your head in a hole and say we are a greatly diverse school, or you can **just be okay with the fact that 74 percent of the school is white**."

Q "I see all types of people walking around campus. **I have friends from all walks of life here**, and it has definitely broadened my horizons to other cultures and backgrounds."

Q "Unfortunately, SMU is a bunch of **upper-class white kids**, with the exception of little pockets of rich minorities and even a smaller pocket of lower-class kids."

Q "At first glance, it's not, but once you get to know people, you realize how different everyone is. **You no longer think of diversity as black and white**."

Q "The campus doesn't look very diverse at first glance, but there are **a lot of clubs and activities that encourage diversity**."

Q "This is an issue of great concern for our campus because it is **very conservative and has a large majority of Caucasians**. There is a lack of equal representation on campus, and a growing divide between the Greeks (usually whites) and the non-Greeks (anyone else). So, I would say it is a bad situation that the school is looking to improve."

Q "Um, I guess. **I don't really look for diversity**."

Q "I think it's a pretty diverse campus. **I see all types of people** when I'm walking to class or around campus."

Q "**This campus is reasonably diverse**, even though sometimes it's like trying to find Waldo. You can meet diverse groups of people to hang out with and be exposed to. It's not just cookie-cutter, upper-class white people."

Q "It has a lot to do with where your school is located. When it comes down to it, **a private university in the South is not going to be diverse**. You have to factor in a lot of other things, like income, too. We're fairly diverse for our location. Having 20 percent minorities in the South is a lot. The student center is the only diverse place on campus. People find their niche here, and they stick to it."

The College Prowler Take On...
Diversity

SMU thrives on its aesthetically-pleasing campus, excellent programs, small classes, and superb funding. The main focus of this school does not revolve around racial diversity. Minorities exist, but they are more difficult to spot than Caucasian students. Most minorities tend to join groups affiliated with their same racial background. In a sense, the school segregates these groups unintentionally. SMU has opened the door for student organizations, and attempts to make each of these groups comfortable. However, in the big picture, these organizations are, perhaps, both a plus and a minus. The best location to find minorities is on the third floor of the student center. Getting involved on campus is a great way to facilitate diversity.

Many students tend to join an organization of some sort within their freshman year, simply to find others that are similar to themselves and foster the same atmosphere they had at home. On the other hand, after a student becomes involved in that particular organization, it becomes more difficult for him or her to branch out of their comfort zone.

C-

The College Prowler® Grade on

Diversity: C-

A high grade in Diversity indicates that ethnic minorities and international students have a notable presence on campus and that students of different economic backgrounds, religious beliefs, and sexual preferences are well-represented.

Guys & Girls

The Lowdown On...
Guys & Girls

Men Undergrads:	Women Undergrads:
45%	55%

Birth Control Available?
Yes. Ladies must first have an exam with either the Health Center's gynecologist or with their own doctor. The prescription can be filled by the Health Center's pharmacy. If a student chooses to use SMU's health insurance policy, she will only have to pay 20 percent of any prescription. The average cost of birth control ranges from $13–$20 per month. The ring, the patch, and oral contraception are offered. Condoms can also be picked up at the Health Center for free.

Most Prevalent STDs on Campus
HPV (human papillomavirus) and herpes are the two most common STDs on campus. Chlamydia and gonorrhea are also present, but they are less frequently diagnosed.

Social Scene
Being socially inept is impossible at SMU because the student body is generally extraverted and amicable. Here in the heart of Texas, rosy cheeks and glistening smiles welcome students on every end of the campus. Students also have an easier time adjusting once they find their niche. The campus is comprised mainly of social butterflies and hospitable people that come from all majors, organizations, and schools. If you were shy upon arrival, you will leave with a pocketful of social skills.

Hookups or Relationships?
During freshman year, dating seems to be the last thing on students' minds. The majority of hookups happen during this time period. Around sophomore year, spring fever sets in, and there are couples popping up all over campus. Students tend to become more committed as they become upperclassmen. But in the beginning, everyone explores and walks on the open playing field. There are, on the other hand, students that have significant others back home or choose not to partake in the exploration.

Best Place to Meet Guys/Girls
Meeting guys and girls on campus is quite simple. As a freshman, the easiest way to meet guys and girls is in the residence halls. Another place to meet people is in the classroom. The class size here forces you to get to know your neighbor. The student center is also an easy target for bumping into new people. Getting involved in an organization facilitates the web of communication here on campus. However, the best place to find hot girls and guys is at parties; whether they are Greek, athletic, or club related. The bar scene is very hip here in Dallas, and it offers a great selection of hotties.

Did You Know?

Top Places to Find Hotties:

1. Greek parties
2. Frat houses
3. Tailgating

Top Places to Hook Up:

1. Dorm rooms
2. Frat houses
3. Random apartments
4. Buses
5. On the dance floor of a bar or club

Dress Code

SMU has a rainbow of designer clothing. Many students sport Ralph Lauren or Lacoste polos. Expensive jeans and Greek T-shirts mix well together. Gucci, Prada, or Chanel sunglasses are paired perfectly with denim miniskirts, polos, and a North Face backpack. The number of girls that roll out of bed and manage to dress themselves decently balances out the number of girls that wake up an hour before class to compose themselves. The dress code here is preppy but laid-back on most days.

Students Speak Out On...
Guys & Girls

"A lot of girls and guys are stuck up rich kids. They've never had a real job and live off their parents for the rest of their college career. The girls are great to look at, but in reality, most of them are fake or have some fake part that daddy paid for."

Q "The girls at SMU are top notch. They wear short, tiny little skirts, and **their wardrobe probably costs more than my car**. Most of the guys are worried about the sun burning their necks and light getting through their aviators at the night club. Most of the frat boys look like they just got off a sailboat."

Q "I don't know about the guys, but **the girls are hot**! But it's more like a museum with pretty pieces that you can't touch."

Q "SMU is considered a very preppy and fashionable school—and for good reason. **Most students have BMWs and wear very expensive clothes everyday**. I don't think this is typical for a college. The girls are very hot, I believe, but unfortunately I can't say the same for my fellow men."

Q "The girls are definitely hot, but they all look the same. The guys all look the same but aren't hot. They all wear the same stuff. **Overall, we're a pretty good-looking campus**."

Q "The girls are hot! **I heard once that we were in _Playboy_ for the hottest girls**. A lot of the girls look like Barbies and as if they just stepped out of a J. Crew catalog. The girls are definitely prissier than the guys. The guys are pretty cool here; they just want to have fun."

Q "The girls are gorgeous, but be prepared. **It doesn't take long to realize that beauty isn't everything**."

Q "The girls are definitely hot at SMU. **There are a lot of wealthy hot chicks**. With money, comes hotties. Rich ones need love, too. A lot of the students here come from well-to-do families, so a lot of girls have high standards. Their designer clothing and expensive jewelry is just eye candy, and they're unattainable. There are a lot of 'normal' girls here, and those people are usually the most fun. At SMU, you just have a higher percentage of prissy teen queens going through their daddy's credit card like it's out of style."

Q "**The guys here are pretty cute**, but a lot of them are pretty immature, too. All the girls here look like they stepped off the pages of _Vogue_. There is plenty of competition for the latest fashions—as well as for boys. Most girls here are nice, but there are some really petty girls here, too."

Q "There are exceptions to everything. Nevertheless, **there are many attractive individuals at this school**."

Q "We definitely have the **prettiest girls in Texas**. That is no joke. About 80 percent of these girls are drop dead gorgeous, but the buck stops there usually. Guys are cool here. They're good looking and have lots of money."

Q "Well, I would like to say that **we are definitely the best-looking university**."

Q "The guys are a weird cross-breed of polite southern men and 'I'm cool because I'm a rich frat kid.' Since there are more girls than guys, I can be ugly, stupid, in a frat, and get the abundance of hot girls to do one night stands. Most of the girls are beautiful—beach babes and southern belles. They are mostly rich. There are some smart, some stupid, some plastic, mostly size two or less. Weren't we ranked in *Playboy* for the hottest girls? **For the most part, everyone is very nice**. That's why I chose to come to SMU. As a high school senior, I walked around campus, and everyone I passed said hello. I didn't even have a name tag."

Q "**The guys can be very cocky at times**. You find a definite mixture between really down-to-earth kids and very cocky people. People here can be very into material things, more so in a name-brand way. At home in Illinois, clothes are just more functional. You buy Birkenstocks because they're comfortable, and they last a long time. People here buy Coach high heels that they'll probably wear twice. People here have very large wardrobes. It's very accessory oriented."

Q "**The girls tend to dress up for class**. I guess it's a southern thing, but most of them do their hair and make up and look pretty put together, even for their 8 a.m. classes."

Q "Most of the guys are the stereotypical frat guy, but not all. If that isn't your thing, **you can easily find guys that you can mix with**. A lot of the girls are also in sororities, but again not all. Most of the students are approachable and very nice. The majority of women are hot."

Q "**The guys are sweet and southern**. Most of them are gentlemen. They are mostly dorky, and clad from head-to-toe in Polo and khaki. The girls are very into their looks, but they are beautiful. Labels, proof of wealth, and social status plague our school."

The College Prowler Take On...
Guys & Girls

SMU has some of the most stunning and beautiful girls from all over the nation. Most of the guys walk around campus with their jaws dragging on the ground, and some of them are even lucky enough to date a couple of SMU's fine and polished ladies. Many of the girls are fashion oriented and fixated on designer labels, such as Gucci, Prada, Burberry, Louis Vuitton, Ralph Lauren, and Dolce and Gabbana. On that note, sadly, the men at SMU are not up to par with the women. It is not out of the ordinary for a girl to date the same attractive guy that her friend has also gone out with. The dating situation at SMU resembles a soap opera. Several students have been around the block, and they have gotten to know their neighbors fairly well (or at least through the magic of gossip). Male students are lucky enough to have eye candy in every single class and in every major.

The campus is changing, though, in respect to an elitist dynamic. There will always be trendy and preppy dressers, but over the course of the last two years, the dress code has been scaled down (thanks to the incoming freshmen). Jeans and T-shirts have become more than acceptable clothing for class, as opposed to polo shirts, khakis, and piles of makeup. There are more and more students sporting the true unkempt "I just woke up" look. Students at SMU, particularly females, have glittering, friendly, attractive, and radiant smiles, which can possibly be attributed to the hospitality of Texas.

B+

The College Prowler® Grade on
Guys: B+

A high grade for Guys indicates that the male population on campus is attractive, smart, friendly, and engaging, and that the school has a decent ratio of guys to girls.

A

The College Prowler® Grade on
Girls: A

A high grade for Girls not only implies that the women on campus are attractive, smart, friendly, and engaging, but also that there is a fair ratio of girls to guys.

Athletics

The Lowdown On...
Athletics

Athletic Division:
NCAA Division I

Conference:
Conference USA

School Mascot
Mustangs

**Males Playing
Varsity Sports:**
253 (9%)

**Females Playing
Varsity Sports:**
198 (6%)

→

Men's Varsity Sports:

Basketball
Cross Country
Football
Golf
Soccer
Swimming & Diving
Tennis

Women's Varsity Sports:

Basketball
Cross Country
Equestrian
Golf
Rowing
Soccer
Swimming & Diving
Tennis
Track & Field
Volleyball

Club Sports:

Badminton
Baseball
Crew
Cricket
Cycling
Fencing
Hockey

(Club Sports, continued)

Mr. and Mrs. SMU Body Building Championship
Graduate Rugby
Judo
Lacrosse
Racquetball
Rock-Climbing
Rugby
Sailing
Soccer
Volleyball

Intramurals:

Basketball
Billiards
Bowling
Dodgeball
Flag Football
Golf Scramble and Tournament
Racquetball (Doubles)
Soccer
Softball
Swim Meet
Table Tennis
Tennis (Singles and Team)
Tug-O-War
Volleyball
Water Polo
Wiffleball

Athletic Fields
Gerald J. Ford Stadium, Westcott Field, Pettus Practice Field

Getting Tickets
Student tickets are unnecessary for most sporting events, such as swimming or diving meets and soccer games. For basketball and football games, a student ticket can be obtained at the actual event or at the Mane Desk in Hughes-Trigg. All tickets and sporting events are free for students. If you have a friend coming to town, it is easy to get them a free ticket as well. Go to the Mane Desk or the ticket office at the event.

Most Popular Sports
If tailgating could be considered a varsity sport, it would be the most populated and all-time favorite event of the general student body. Football generally receives the highest attendance by students, especially since tailgating precedes the game. All the other sports tend to have their regular followers, but their attendance is nowhere near that of football's.

Overlooked Teams
The soccer team, along with the swimming and diving team, do not receive the attention they deserve. Both have been ranked within the top 25 teams in the nation, and they improve every year. However, many students still choose not to attend.

Best Place to Take a Walk
White Rock Lake, Sorority Park (because there is a playground), the school (thanks to the plethora of greenery), in the residential neighborhoods surrounding the school.

Gyms/Facilities

Cinco Center

Currently the Cinco Center resembles a small shed and does not accommodate enough people. Students have to find a certain time slot in order to comfortably work out and be able to use the gym equipment. A newer and larger gym is under construction and will be more realistic in fulfilling the students' needs.

Dedman Center

The Dedman Center is also a part of the renovation going on that involves a new gym. Both will be connected. At the moment, though, the Dedman Center is the home of indoor basketball, volleyball, badminton, racquetball and handball courts, tracks, several tennis courts, and a climbing wall. The first phase of renovations has been completed, and more improvements are yet to come. The Dedman Center is also the home of drop-in fitness classes that offer yoga and aerobics. Once the new facility is completely erected, most students will have no problem finding a place to work out.

> "Varsity sports are not big at all. No one really knows or cares about them. Intramural sports are great, but Greeks are mainly involved."

Q "We have a great soccer team and swimming team, but **no one cares about sports**. Football is awful. They spend more and more money to get better, but all they do is help the players drive nicer cars. We have the potential to be excited about sports but lack the motivation from the players and the crowds. Intramural sports are fun. They are huge among frats and sororities."

Q "**Sports aren't as big a deal as the parties before and after the games**. We may not have won a game last year, but our tailgating skills are unmatched."

Q "**Both varsity and intramural sports are pretty big**. IM sports, especially between fraternities, are very popular. The varsity sports are kind of quiet, with the exception of football. SMU is home to some world-class caliber athletes. We've had members of the swim team competing in the Olympics. The NCAA tournament for soccer was hosted here. The school really tries to encourage football spirit and attendance, but honestly, it's really hard to get past the tailgate and see your school lose a lot. It is improving, though. The games are still fun to go to because it's still a college football team, and the stadium is nice."

Q "Varsity sports, as far as I can tell, are not all that big. IM sports seem to be **very popular with clubs and Greek life**."

Q "Varsity **sports aren't that huge a deal here**, especially since our football team stinks. If our football team was better, I think a lot more people would have school pride. I know we have a good soccer team, but no one around here cares about soccer. IM sports are a huge deal in the frat league."

Q "Varsity sports are struggling presently, but there is always hope, right? A lot of people sign up for intramural sports. **It's a great way to meet people and get exercise at the same time**."

Q "Some varsity sports on campus are bigger than others. Results and rankings are not a determining factor for attendance. **Soccer and swimming have high rankings, but not many people attend the matches or meets**."

Q "**Sports are big here, especially football**. And almost everybody does IM sports."

Q "**We love to tailgate for football**, and we'll go to a bit of the game. Soccer gets a lot of fans and so does basketball. IM sports are fun, and a lot of people participate, especially Greek groups."

Q "**Even though the football team has had winless seasons, people still came out to the games**. Basketball is also big. All of the other sports do not get enough attention. IM sports are a great way to have fun and compete in sports that you like, or want to try out. Usually, the dorm that you are staying in will organize some kind of IM team."

Q "I do not really follow sports beyond the tailgate parties, which are awesome. **The sports are a joke, really**."

Q "Varsity sports are very big (soccer, football, and basketball are the biggest). **Intramurals are dominated by the Greeks**, so there is somewhat of a divide there; they are still very big, though."

Q "Football may not be a great program, but there are so many programs at the top of the NCAA rankings. I don't think getting a great football team will rush the fans to the stadium either. **People leave the game at half-time even though we are winning**. Having a great football team would draw crowds from outside of SMU and increase athletic revenue."

The College Prowler Take On...
Athletics

SMU is still attempting to recover from the football saga of 1987, where the NCAA punished SMU's football team with the "death penalty," sanctioning the team for one year. SMU has had several setbacks within the past two decades. The school has joined the Western Athletic Conference, changed coaches, and moved to a new stadium. Recently, SMU saw its first win in the fourth game of the season and experienced the ritual of taking down the goal posts for the first time. This may seem a bit overdramatic for other schools that are used to going home happy, but for SMU, it was a milestone. Faith in the team and attendance may finally have a chance.

Where there's a will, there's a way . . . well, maybe to tailgate incessantly. SMU is home to some of the top teams in the nation, yet the majority of students would rather check out the weekend bar specials than actually go to a sporting event. In the past, some of the school's athletes competed in the Olympics. It is surprising that the athletes are doing so well, because if they were to look up into the stands, they might become discouraged by such a low turnout. Football only stands a chance because there is somewhat of a pre-party before the game with tailgating. Maybe if $1 beer specials were offered to students at all sporting events, the attendance would not be so depressing. The ability to be a sports-oriented school is on the tips of the students' fingers, but SMU is still waiting for the students to rise to the occasion.

C+

The College Prowler® Grade on
Athletics: C+

A high grade in Athletics indicates that students have school spirit, that sports programs are respected, that games are well-attended, and that intramurals are a prominent part of student life.

Nightlife

The Lowdown On...
Nightlife

Club and Bar Prowler:
Popular Nightlife Spots!

Club Crawler:

The clubs and bars in Dallas cater mainly to Dallas professionals and trendy 20-somethings. Nightlife varies by area. The more sophisticated bars are located in West Village, whereas the jeans-and-a-T-shirt bars are on Greenville Avenue and Yale Boulevard.

(Club Crawler, continued)

Most of the bars close at 2 a.m., but on Saturdays, clubs in Deep Ellum shut their doors at 4 a.m. If you are under 21, you will be branded with black "Xs" on each hand. For an SMU student, Dallas has a great variety of bars to try, and eventually, you will find your favorite ones.

→

Bar Prowler:

Al-Amir

7402 Greenville
Avenue, #101

(214) 739-2647

*www.alamirdallas.net
/home.html*

Al-Amir is not only able
to showcase excellent
Lebanese food, but it also
has a great nightlife scene.
The building itself seems
like a maze because there
are several different dance
areas above and below the
main entrance. There is a DJ
that plays multicultural dance
music, and at 9:30 p.m.,
there are authentic Middle
Eastern belly dancers. Upon
entering the club, you will
notice a fountain as well as a
gazebo, where you can eat
and partake in the hookah
experience. You must be
eighteen to be admitted and
of-age to drink. There is a
cover charge if you are 21.

Chaucer's International

5321 E. Mockingbird
Lane, Suite 240;
Mockingbird Station

www.chaucersrestaurant.com

Located on the second floor
of Mockingbird Station,
Chaucer's is a new SMU
favorite. During the day, it is
an elegant restaurant, and
by nighttime, the restaurant
appeal diminishes while the
bar rapidly fills up. The dark
indoor setting is somewhat
intimate with several polished
wooden tables for people to
relax. There is a tiny dance
floor accompanied by the
latest music, but most of
the students will be found
dancing their way towards the
bartender. There are several
tables outside as well, and
this is where most students
socialize. Since it is a college-
oriented bar, the dress code
is hip and trendy, however,
most people tend to wear
jeans. You must be 18 to get
in, but of-age to drink. There
is no cover charge.

Homebar

5627 Dyer Street

www.thehomebar.net

Home Bar is run by the owners of the former Green Elephant, which was an SMU favorite. For large parties, you can rent out the entire venue of Homebar. This can be free, or cost up to $500, depending on the day, time, and type of party. There are two bars, lounge areas, and an outdoor stage with seating. While a lot of students miss the Green Elephant, Homebar is beginning to fill that void.

Jack's Pub & Volleyball Club

5550 Yale Boulevard

(214) 360-0999

www.jackspub.com

Another casual SMU hangout, Jack's Pub features four outdoor white sand volleyball courts. The courts are also illuminated at nighttime. Inside there is a tiny dance floor and several booths around the bar. Domino with 106.7 KDL is there on Mondays to get the party started. Jack's Pub is just a block away from SMU, so

(Jack's Pub, continued)

after a long day of classes, students come here to sit down with their friends and enjoy pitchers. You must be 18 to get in and of-age to drink.

Margarita Ranch

5321 E. Mockingbird Lane, Suite 110; Mockingbird Station

(214) 824-3573

www.margaritaranch.com

Margarita Ranch is Mockingbird Station's other college moneymaker. The bar/restaurant is located on the ground level near Chaucer's. Quiet and charming on the inside, Margarita Ranch is a great place to just sit down with friends and enjoy different types of margaritas. Margarita Ranch is preferred for late night because of the free chips and salsa. There is also an outdoor patio area. The dress code is hip and trendy, but casual in the sense that nice jeans can be worn. Just recently, Margarita Ranch lowered the age to 18 for admission; however, you must still be of-age to drink.

The Samba Room

4514 Travis St.

(214) 522-4137

The Samba Room is a great spot for the modern, stylish, upbeat students at SMU. It can be fairly expensive, but the lively music and atmosphere is a big draw for students. Specialty drinks like the mojito are a must-have at this place.

The San Francisco Rose

3024 Greenville Avenue

(214) 826-2020

For a more chill and laid-back atmosphere, the "Rose" is the place to be. Your chances of getting the evil eye for wearing jeans and a T-shirt are much lower here than at other bars. The setting is comfortable: there is a jukebox, an old telephone booth, big screen televisions, and several pictures adorning the walls. There is also an outdoor patio. You must be 21 to drink and make it past the bouncer.

Trinity Hall

5321 E. Mockingbird Lane

(214) 887-3600

For the traditional Irish experience, students head to Trinity Hall for beers, whiskey, and great Irish food. Trinity Hall offers nightly entertainment like pub quizzes, poker nights, and live music. Every Tuesday is Tasting Tuesday. Throughout the month, you can sip different whiskies, wines, and beers, depending on the week. They also offer PPV rugby and soccer matches.

Student Favorites:

Chaucer's

Jack's Pub

Margarita Ranch

The San Francisco Rose

Other Places to Check Out:

The Candle Room

Club Blue

Club Nikita

The Ginger Man

The Granada Theater

Gyspy Tea Room

Mike's Treehouse

Ozona's Bar & Grill

Suede Bar & Grill

Bars Close At:

2 a.m.

Favorite Drinking Games

Beer Pong

Card Games (A$$hole)

Century Club

Power Hour

Quarters

Useful Resources for Nightlife:

Daily Campus

Dallas Observer

Dallas Morning News

Quick

www.guidelive.com

Primary Areas with Nightlife:

Deep Ellum

Downtown

Greenville Avenue

Mockingbird Station

SMU/Yale Boulevard

West Village

Cheapest Place to Get a Drink:

Chaucer's

Local Specialties:

The frozen margarita (originally created here in Dallas)

What to Do if You're Not 21

Curtain Club/Liquid Lounge
2800 Main Street
Deep Ellum

(214) 742-2336

www.curtainclub.com

Curtain Club and Liquid Lounge are well-known for live music. Local musicians and regional bands frequent both venues. If you enjoy kicking back and chilling out to live music, this is the place for you. Wear comfortable shoes because you will be standing the entire time. The calendar of performers is listed online. The doors open at 9 p.m. for anyone under 21. There is a small charge of $3 unless there is a big concert, then the fee is a bit higher.

Other music venues that are 18-and-over
Across the Street Bar, the Granada, Lakeview Theater, Trees

Organization Parties

Several of the organizations on campus will rent out restaurants/bars and clubs for private parties. Most of them are all Greek. Although you may not be able to get on the bus to the party because they are lists-only, you can drive yourself there and still reap the benefits of nightlife. Fraternities and sororities pair up and host events at different venues together or separately. As a freshman, you will be introduced to the bars and clubs through these parties. Greek parties contain the highest number of students.

Frats

See the Greek Section!

Students Speak Out On...
Nightlife

> "The parties on campus are awesome, although you have to be Greek and a girl to go to most of them. We have a bus system that takes us to and from parties, which is pretty safe."

Q "**The only parties on campus are fraternity or sorority** parties, and personally, they get old really quick. The fun bars off campus are 10, Nikita, the Samba Room, or pretty much anything on lower Greenville or in Deep Ellum. If it is school bars you want, you can go to Mike's Tree House, but sometimes it is good to not see SMU people everywhere."

Q "The parties are great, but **only if you are involved in Greek life**."

Q "The problem with SMU and on-campus parties is that **the school is terrified of the idea of liability**. As opposed to regulating on-campus parties, they would much rather thrust the responsibility onto the students themselves by making them ride buses. This leads to drunk driving, especially since the buses have lists. No matter how many speeches and laws that are enforced, drinking in college is here to stay. It's disappointing that the school chooses to remain naïve."

Q "The good thing about our school is that **there is always a party somewhere**. You can always find a place to go hang out with your friends and drink. There are so many bars down Greenville and at Mockingbird Station. Finding a party scene is not that hard. Everyone loves Chaucer's!"

Q "Greek parties are the parties to go to both on and off campus. There are bars very close to campus, like on Greenville. **The drinks are reasonably priced, and the atmosphere at most bars is relaxed and fun**. Suede and the Rose are hot spots."

Q "The parties on campus are okay. The **bars and clubs are great off campus**. Most of the best clubs are 21-and-up, though."

Q "Parties, well I'm not sure how to put that, except '**all the time**,' and 'what's class?'"

Q "On-campus parties are okay. It is basically **a bunch of people getting drunk and talking to each other over loud music**. The bus parties are cool. It's clubbing for free, with a lot of getting drunk there, too. Good bars are Trinity Hall, Jacks Pub, and Ozona's."

Q "**The parties are pretty good**. They are Greek dominated. The bars, well, I'm spoiled because I have friends with connections to the Candle Room, which I enjoy since it's upscale but laid-back. The best bar in Mockingbird Station is Spike. They have the best mixed drinks since the fruit mix is hand squeezed instead of just using syrup. Club Blue is fun. The Samba Room is great for pre-drinks. The Latin dance club across from the Samba Room is fun, too."

Q "Parties are always fun. You get on a bus, and they take you to the place where the party is. **There are always parties going on at the fraternity houses**. One bar that people go to is Bar X (10) because it's close, and on the 10th, they have ten-cent drinks."

Q "**SMU is very much a party school**. Starting on Wednesday, you can find a party easily; especially on Thursdays (the beginning of the college weekend). Most are frat parties, which require being on a list, but all you need is to know people. You can also go bar hopping. Jack's Pub has a good environment and beach volleyball. Lower Greenville is also a good place to hang out."

Q "I am going to be a senior, so I hang out with an older crowd. The fraternity parties are always a blast and a great way to make new friends. I met many of my friends and even my last boyfriend there. I have outgrown the theme parties, so **I prefer bars like the San Francisco Rose**, where I know everyone. If I want to escape SMU, I relax at the Ginger Man in a different neighborhood."

Q "**The parties on campus are dominated by Greek life**. Not being a member of Greek life is definitely a handicap if you are looking into partying on campus. Off-campus bars and clubs are really fun but nothing like you would find in, say, Boston or New Orleans."

The College Prowler Take On...
Nightlife

In the beginning, the possibilities for going out seem nonexistent and as if there is nothing to do but hang out in the Greek life arena. But Dallas has several well-known and eclectic venues tucked away all over the city. The major nightlife scene caters to an older and more sophisticated crowd, and the only challenge is to avoid becoming comfortable in the same bars and clubs—keep trying new ones! Students tend to find their favorite nightlife spots and hold tight until they graduate. For those who are under the drinking age and enjoy live music, there are music spots not far from campus, such as the Granada and the Gypsy Tea Room, which host bands on a nightly basis. If you're really feeling adventurous, head down to Deep Ellum and walk the enormous strip of clubs. Most only require a small cover charge to get in, and there are a number of clubs specifically for people under 21. But turning 21 changes everything. It not only means that you can get into the SMU favorites, like Chaucer's and Margarita Ranch, but that you can actually legally partake in the fervor of getting wasted.

For freshmen girls, frat parties are great because it's free beer and a close walk home. On the weekends though, the campus becomes completely desolate, minus the buses for Greek parties. Other groups, such as athletes, partake in the social scene and throw a few of the biggest parties aside from Greeks. There are also always parties in people's homes, so there is no reason to ever complain that there is nothing to do on a Friday night. This school offers a brilliant networking system, both on the career side and unintentionally through nightlife. Whether you are relaxing with a movie, some friends, and beer, or out at a club or bar, going to all different kinds of parties is the best way to meet new people.

A-

The College Prowler® Grade on

Nightlife: A-

A high grade in Nightlife indicates that there are many bars and clubs in the area that are easily accessible and affordable. Other determining factors include the number of options for the under-21 crowd and the prevalence of house parties.

Greek Life

The Lowdown On...
Greek Life

Number of Fraternities:
11

Undergrad Men in Fraternities:
34%

Number of Sororities:
11

Undergrad Women in Sororities:
47%

→

Fraternities on Campus:

Beta Theta Pi
Kappa Alpha Order
Kappa Alpha Psi
Kappa Sigma
Lambda Chi Alpha
Phi Delta Theta
Phi Gamma Delta
Pi Kappa Alpha
Sigma Alpha Epsilon
Sigma Chi
Sigma Phi Epsilon

Sororities on Campus:

Alpha Chi Omega
Alpha Kappa Alpha
Chi Omega
Delta Delta Delta
Delta Gamma
Delta Sigma Theta
Gamma Phi Beta
Kappa Alpha Theta
Kappa Kappa Gamma
Pi Beta Phi
Zeta Phi Beta

Multicultural Colonies:

Alpha Psi Lambda
Delta Lambda Phi
Kappa Delta Chi
National Social Fraternity
Omega Delta Phi
Sigma Lambda Gamma

Other Greek Organizations:

Interfraternity Council
Multicultural Greek Council
National Pan-Hellenic Council
Pan-Hellenic Council

Did You Know?

Each semester, Greek organizations pair up and participate in **Talent Show** during Family Weekend in the fall, and Sing Song during Mother's/Father's Weekend in the spring.

In the fall, fraternities and sororities build and **present floats for the homecoming parade** and they compete for first, second, or third place. Most of the homecoming king and queen nominees are Greek.

SMU participates in **deferred rush**, which means that recruitment takes place during the last week of the holiday break.

Students Speak Out On...
Greek Life

"**Greek life is very present at this school. I would say that it borders on domination of the social scene.**"

Q "**Greeks take over everything**. You cannot hide."

Q "Sororities pay for status. They're so pointless in comparison to fraternities. Girls pay huge dues and don't reap the same benefits as guys. You don't see the same dispersal of money with sororities as you do with fraternities. It doesn't dominate the school, but **it has a definite presence in the social scene**. Greeks have the parties on the weekend. It's worth it to join, if you meet the right people. You're by no means ruled out of Greek life if you don't join."

Q "I'd say that Greek life is a big deal on campus, but it doesn't dominate the social scene. **It's only a big deal if you care**. Most parties are open, and there is plenty of other stuff to do as well."

Q "**It's just a way for people to exclude others and feel more elite**. I have my own group, so I can exclude them. If I didn't have a group, I would definitely say yes, Greek life rules the social scene. I think Greek life dominates SMU because a lot of people go out and buy a keg, come up with a name of a party, but don't charge you admission. This just reels freshmen into wanting to be in that elite little group so they can be the center of the party."

Q "**The Greek scene is most definitely huge at SMU**. Most of the parties are facilitated by sororities and fraternities. Greek life heavily dominates this campus. There doesn't seem to be too much distaste for independence and likewise. Greek life has a huge part to play on campus and in the student legislature."

Q "Greek life is huge here and definitely overtakes the social scene, but **that doesn't mean just because you're not affiliated**, you can't have a good time. I would advise people to have an open mind about it. At first I was against it, but then I looked into it more and changed my mind."

Q "I would highly encourage Greek life **if you want a busy social life**."

Q "I love Greek life. It's fun and exciting. **I like the secrets, the parties, and the freshmen girls**. So many people are Greek, and if you're not, that's okay because you know so many people that are. You make instant friends and social connections for after college. It makes it fun to go to other cities because you can visit all the other chapters' houses. It definitely takes over the social scene, though."

Q "**Even though not everyone is Greek, it feels like it**. It totally dominates the campus."

Q "Most of the parties are Greek. **It's not necessary to be a member to attend some of their activities**, though. The parties are usually off campus at nifty bars and themed. The school supports safety, and uses buses to prevent drunk driving, which I think is way cool."

Q "**You have to be Greek to have a social life**. Everything revolves around fraternities and sororities."

Q "You are not overwhelmed by Greek life, but **it is extremely easy to get into**. The frats and sororities are nice in general, especially if you find the non-hazing ones. Most parties are Greek related, so if partying is your thing, then go Greek."

Q "Having a Greek system helps our school. **It gives everyone something to do**."

Q "**Greek life dominates the social scene**, and, most of the time, on-campus activities such as student government and other clubs."

The College Prowler Take On...
Greek Life

New students foreign to the Greek system will be stunned by the phenomenon created by the fraternities and sororities here on campus. Greek life feeds directly into the community created by SMU with its small student population and functions as the primary way of life—well, at least socially. On the other hand, while people may assume what they will about Greek life and attach certain labels to it (such as elitism and "buying your friends"), most will soon find themselves amongst the crowd, either by joining it or making friends who participate in it. Being Greek allows you instant access into theme parties that are held every weekend. Most Greeks are proud that they are a part of an organization, but by no means will they treat you differently because you are not Greek . . . you just won't be able to get into most of the parties. Because SMU is in the South, recruitment is an immense ordeal, and quite a bit of emphasis is placed on the entire scene.

Every day, different colored jerseys are visible all over campus, in addition to Greek T-shirts that everyone wears to class. Girls are also equipped with buttons on their purses and backpacks. But once again, Greek life does not take over the entire campus. It's just highly noticeable. On the flip side, the percentage of students joining fraternities and sororities is slowly dwindling. Don't make assumptions about the people or the system; check it out and judge for yourself.

A-

The College Prowler® Grade on

Greek Life: A-

A high grade in Greek Life indicates that sororities and fraternities are not only present, but also active on campus. Other determining factors include the variety of houses available and the respect the Greek community receives from the rest of the campus.

Drug Scene

The Lowdown On...
Drug Scene

Most Prevalent Drugs on Campus:
Adderall, Alcohol, Marijuana

Liquor-Related Referrals:
180

Liquor-Related Arrests:
120

Drug-Related Referrals:
26

Drug-Related Arrests:
10

Drug Counseling Programs

Memorial Health Center

(214) 768-4021

Services: Alcohol and drug assessment, intervention, short-term counseling, referral to other outside help, spreads campus awareness via student organizations, offers support groups both on and off campus, educates students through a mandatory wellness class and offers Substance Abuse Awareness Classes, surveys students to find the average use of drugs and alcohol, offers a peer education group (BACCHUS), EChug online screening

Alcoholics Anonymous

Neuhoff Catholic Student Center

(214) 987-0044

Services: Open student meeting that meets Mondays, Wednesdays, and Fridays at noon

Central Group

1810 Hall Street

Services: Local meetings every day for narcotics users

Students Speak Out On...
Drug Scene

{
"Of course they're here. If you want something, you can get it. Drugs are prevalent here, especially pot and coke."

Q "It just depends, really. **A lot of people do them, and a lot of people don't**."

Q "It's definitely there. **It's not in your face**. I imagine it's not larger than any other college. It won't come out to get you. There is a drug scene, but if you want to stay away from drugs, you will have no problem doing so."

Q "**There are drugs on every campus, and this one is no different**. But you usually don't see it out at parties. I think people's drug use here is usually pretty private."

Q "A few kids smoke pot. **Some of the real rich kids are cokeheads**. Mostly, we're all just a bunch of binge drinkers."

Q "It is just as existent as any other school, neither worse nor better. **I see a lot of prescription drug abuse** rather than street drugs."

Q "**Adderall seems to be the new study drug**, and I think people from every group or type can be prone to using it. Party drugs like cocaine seem to be popular among some of the more upper-class Greek people on campus. And who can forget GHB? It's popular among the frat boys for sex assistance."

Q "It's there. It's very accessible. It's pretty hush. **There are more drugs than it seems**."

Q "**I haven't seen hardly any drug use**, but I know that it goes on."

Q "**The drug scene is pretty underground**. Other than smoking and drinking, which is blatantly obvious, other forms of drugs are just heard about."

Q "**Anything you want is pretty readily available**. Some circles get pretty out of hand, mostly with cocaine; but you can escape it just as easily as you can find it."

Q "**I have heard about cocaine being a big issue**, but I haven't encountered it myself."

Drug Scene

No college can escape the scourge of drugs and alcohol. It is an integrated part of the whole college experience. The challenge, on that note, is to regulate the usage so that students are able to safely enjoy their four years of irresponsibility. SMU is similar to every typical college; it has drug users and alcoholics. You can get access to any kind of drug you wish. The most prevalent drugs are marijuana and Adderall. Students typically only use Adderall in moderation, to cram for tests and exams. Another drug you may encounter, by rumors specifically, is cocaine. The coke scene is completely underground—along with all other hardcore drugs. The most blatant drug on campus is alcohol. Every semester there are posters all over campus with statistics and other little factoids to help educate students on drug usage. Other illegal drugs tend to be concealed, and the usage is marginal.

Students are more addicted to having fun with their friends at a bar with a few beers, rather than kicking back in an apartment and shooting heroin. On the surface, this campus is drug-free—minus the few stoners and fans of bar specials found on every campus.

C-

The College Prowler® Grade on

Drug Scene: C-

A high grade in the Drug Scene indicates that drugs are not a noticeable part of campus life; drug use is not visible, and no pressure to use them seems to exist.

Campus Strictness

The Lowdown On...
Campus Strictness

What Are You Most Likely to Get Caught Doing on Campus?
- Underage drinking (in dorms, too)
- Parking in an undesignated spot
- Walking home drunk late at night
- Having loud parties
- Running stop signs
- Having candles and extension cords in your dorm room
- Drinking illegally on the Boulevard during tailgate
- Stumbling off of a bus intoxicated
- Urinating on campus or public indecency
- Cheating on a test
- Driving into a curb or median while drunk

Students Speak Out On...
Campus Strictness

"They're very strict on any drugs and moderate on drinking. If it is a problem, they will give you a ticket. Otherwise, they know it's college, and they try to make sure everyone is safe at the end of the day."

Q "SMU PD is pretty strict. **They take drugs and drinking quite seriously**. It's not to a ridiculous extent. Drugs are punished very severely on campus. As far as drinking goes, cops will use their own judgment on how to evaluate the situation. They're not going to crack down on the tiniest infractions."

Q "**It all depends on who catches you**, where and when you are caught, and how many times you've been caught before."

Q "**If a cop knows you're doing something wrong, he or she won't let you get away with it**. The moral of the story is this: If you're planning on doing something you shouldn't be, don't do it. And if you do, be smart about it. Sometimes you can get in trouble just for being in the wrong place at the wrong time."

Q "**I never feel like I'm going to get in trouble**. I seriously don't think anyone can get into real trouble. We have cops at our parties. They control it."

Q "You don't want to be caught with either drugs or alcohol. **You most likely won't get off with just a warning**, so don't push your luck."

Q "I wish we had security guards like at every other college in the U.S. **I don't think the police are easy on anyone**. They just haven't gotten around to catching those people, or they are too busy working with the really drunk people or heavy drug abusers."

Q "It depends on if you're stupid. Kids will be kids, and drugs and drinking will happen. **If you're not cautious though, you will get busted**, and you'll at least get a ticket and a hearing."

Q "**If you're underage, they usually let you go with a warning**. On the other hand, if you do get caught, the punishment is typically spending a Saturday learning about drugs and alcohol."

Q "If you get caught, they're strict, but **if you are careful enough, you can get away with almost anything**."

Q "The police are very strict with drinking and drugs, but **they tolerate kids drinking in moderation** rather than binge drinking."

Campus Strictness

SMU PD is lenient with students and drinking on campus—to an extent. If you are carrying a bottle of beer around a party, they will kindly suggest that you pour the beer into a plastic cup. If you pass out at a party somewhere, or seem belligerent, they will no longer give you the blind eye. The campus police will take care of you and make sure that you are safe. Students belittle the SMU PD but forget that they are just doing their job. The simplest rule to follow is this: practice good judgment. This means you should make sure your door in your dorm room is closed before you start crushing cans on your head. Don't get into a car with a drunk driver, because you can be guilty just by association. Walk off the bus—don't tumble. Avoid carrying open containers anywhere on campus. And finally, lock up your liquor!

The campus police are aware that students are young and away from home and will make poor decisions every now and then. They act as the fun aunt or uncle from back home that will take care of you, but refrain from telling your parents about your minor offense. Once you step out of the realm of small offenses, it is an entirely different ball game. It is common for an SMU student to have one alcohol violation, but most never receive a second one.

B

The College Prowler® Grade on

Campus
Strictness: B

A high Campus Strictness grade implies an overall lenient atmosphere; police and RAs are fairly tolerant, and the administration's rules are flexible.

Parking

The Lowdown On...
Parking

Approximate Parking Permit Cost:

$200 per year

SMU Parking Services:

(214) 768-7275

*www.smu.edu/pd/parking/
parkingrules.asp*

Student Parking Lot?

Yes

Freshmen Allowed to Park?

Yes

Parking Permits:

Every student and faculty member can obtain a parking permit easily. First, pre-pay for the permit online at *access.smu.edu*, and then proceed to the Park N' Pony office on the second floor of Hughes-Trigg with a valid driver's license and license plate number.

Common Parking Tickets:

Expired Meter: $25
No Parking Zone: $30
Handicapped Zone: $200
Fire Lane: $50

Did You Know?

Best Places to Find a Parking Spot

- The meters behind Fondren Library, but only if you do not have a permit.

- Along the residential streets off of Airline.

- Any place that freshman girls can park, if you can somehow manage to get that permit.

- The parking garages, after 3 p.m., when most classes end.

- Faculty/staff lots after 5 p.m. and on weekends, but only if they are not marked specifically "24-hours."

Good Luck Getting a Parking Spot Here!

Hughes-Trigg before 4 p.m. and the Airline Garage

The Boot!

After your sixth parking violation, your car will be branded with a bright yellow boot each time you receive a ticket. Ouch!

Students Speak Out On...
Parking

"Parking needs a lot of improvement here. And if you are a freshman boy, you will be hiking out to the farthest parking lot every day. For girls and upperclassmen, parking is more tolerable."

Q "Don't we pay enough for this school already? I would rather they just attach $100 to my tuition and **leave my car alone or use the money to build another parking lot**."

Q "**It is easy to park**. It just depends on where you want to park and where you can prevent getting a ticket. SMU police will ticket you!"

Q "**Parking is a headache**, especially if you live off campus and get to school after 10 a.m."

Q "**If you're not a freshman guy, parking is not that bad**. SMU totally screws over the freshmen guys by putting them on the farthest corners of the campus. I think it's a poor decision, because it's so close to the highway. By the time a cop responds to your call, someone has taken off with your stereo already. On the other hand, there are so many students here, that I don't think there is anywhere else to park."

Q "**Parking here is the worst**. I hate it. It takes you 30 minutes just to find a vacant spot."

Q "**There are always too many cars** and not enough spaces."

Q "The parking is horrible. **Tickets are only $25, though**."

Q "Parking blows here! **Construction hinders parking**. Right now they're redoing Dedman, so the freshman male parking lot is closed, and they have to park elsewhere and take up more spots. If you're off campus, you have to plan for an extra 20–30 minutes just to find a spot so you won't be late to class. SMU needs more parking garages."

Q "**Actually, it's hard to park**. Everyone drives on this campus. There aren't enough parking garages, and you do have to walk really far to class."

Q "Practically everyone drives to campus or has a car, so **parking can be messy**. However, they do have a few parking garages, so it's not that hard to find a spot."

Q "If you live on campus, it isn't much of an issue. **There are parking garages located within five minutes by foot from almost any dorm**. If you live off campus, you may not get a parking spot sometimes."

Q "Campus parking is a mess. **Fines are dished out limitlessly, because everyone illegally parks**, and everyone illegally parks because there isn't any space on campus."

The College Prowler Take On...
Parking

SMU does not guarantee a spot to every student that purchases a parking permit. Parking spots function on convenience. The early bird gets his worm—or spot rather. Students constantly complain about never finding a parking spot. Even the students with the best permit (yellow for first-year women or Greeks living in the houses) have difficulty parking. Most will circle around a parking area three times before parking far away in a garage—especially freshmen males. During the day, the garages are packed, and you should consider yourself lucky if you get a spot on the rooftop (fifth level). And if you think you're slick and turn your flashers on briefly even though you're parked illegally, don't be surprised if you receive a ticket. Students receive more parking tickets than alcohol violations.

The easiest way to find a parking spot is to take a couple aspirin before you get in your car, and plan for about 30 minutes to find a spot if you live off campus. If you're parking in the garages, don't be dismayed if the sign reads "Lot Full," because it is never correct. Parking is a cinch for those students who have class at 8 a.m.

D

The College Prowler® Grade on

Parking: D

A high grade in this section indicates that parking is both available and affordable, and that parking enforcement isn't overly severe.

Transportation

The Lowdown On...
Transportation

Ways to Get Around Town:

On Campus

SMU Escort Service
Giddy-Up (24-hours)

(214) 768-3333

Public Transportation

Dallas Area Rapid Transit (DART)

(214) 979-1111

Get bus schedules at *www. dart.org* or from the Perkins Administration Building

Taxi Cabs

Star Cab (214) 252-0055

Classic Cab (972) 233-6003

DFW Transportation
(214) 468-8448

Best Ways to Get Around Town

Borrow a friend's car

Invest in a bike

Take a hike

Take the DART for free by using your SMU Transit Pass

Car Rentals

Alamo
local: (214) 351-0741;
national: (800) 327-9633,
www.alamo.com

Avis
local: (214) 357-1711;
national: (800) 831-2847,
www.avis.com

Budget
local: (214) 353-4940;
national: (800) 527-0700,
www.budget.com

Dollar
local: (866) 434-2226;
national: (800) 800-4000,
www.dollar.com

Enterprise
local: (214) 366-9591;
national: (800) 736-8222,
www.enterprise.com

Hertz
local: (214) 634-7832;
national: (800) 654-3131,
www.hertz.com

National
local: (214) 357-0478;
national: (800) 227-7368,
www.nationalcar.com

Ways to Get Out of Town:

Airlines Serving Dallas

American Airlines
(800) 433-7300
www.americanairlines.com

Continental
(800) 523-3273
www.continental.com

Delta
(800) 221-1212
www.delta-air.com

Northwest
(800) 225-2525
www.nwa.com

Southwest
(800) 435-9792
www.southwest.com

United
(800) 241-6522
www.united.com

US Airways
(800) 428-4322
www.usairways.com

Airport

Dallas Love Field

(214) 670-6073

Dallas Love Field is a mere five miles from campus, and it's no more than a 10-minute drive. However, there are only two carriers at this airport: Southwest and Continental.

Dallas/Fort Worth
International Airport
(972) 574-8888

DFW is approximately 22
miles away and 30 minutes
driving time from SMU.

How to Get There

Super Shuttle
(817) 329-2000. This shuttle
offers SMU students a
discounted rate of $22.75
one way to DFW, and $20.75
one way to Love Field.

Yellow Checker Shuttle
(214) 841-1900. This shuttle
also offers a special rate for
SMU students: $22 to DFW
and $18 to Love Field.

A cab ride to the DFW airport
costs about $40. To Love
Field, it's about $15.

Greyhound

The Greyhound Terminal is
located in downtown Dallas
five miles from campus. For
schedule information, call
(800) 454-2487.

www.greyhound.com

Dallas Greyhound Terminal
205 S. Lamar
Dallas, TX 75202
(214) 655-7082

Amtrak

The Amtrak Train Station
is located in downtown
Dallas approximately six
miles from SMU.

For schedule information, call
(800) 872-7245.

www.amtrak.com

Dallas Amtrak Train Station
400 South Houston Street
Dallas, TX 75202
(214) 653-1101

Travel Agents

Rudi Steele Travel, Inc.
Highland Park Village
(214) 522-2777

www.rudisteele.com

D-FW Tours
LBJ Freeway
(972) 980-4540

www.dfwtours.com

Ultima Travel, Inc.
McKinney Avenue
(214) 922-9255

www.ultima-travel.com

Students Speak Out On...
Transportation

> "There are buses going everywhere out of Mockingbird Station. You will need a PhD in public transportation to figure out how to get from point A to point B because it's confusing."

Q "It's nonexistent. **You can't feel comfortable using public transportation** without feeling like an outcast or being scared."

Q "**It is not convenient** if you need to get around Dallas."

Q "Transportation is **not easy at all**. The bus does not come on campus on the weekends."

Q "**It takes a bit of work, but it can be done**. There is a shuttle that comes to campus and takes students (and anyone else) to the DART station near school."

Q "I don't really know. I know there is a DART system and Mustang Express locally. SMU also provides SMU Rides, a free taxi service for students, which is included in your tuition. **It's not a huge thing that people use**, but there are some that use these services."

Q "**I've never used it**, and I don't know anyone that does."

Q "**The DART is awesome and available**, but no one takes advantage of it!"

Q "I don't think it's that convenient, but **SMU has tried to make it easier by providing free passes to DART** and by offering buses to campus."

Q "Public transportation is improving, but it is useful to know someone with a car. **You should not depend on the buses**, or any other forms of public transportation, in Dallas."

Q "**It is actually pretty convenient**. I have even ridden the bus! I have never seen one other SMU student use it, though. You don't really need it because everything is practically on campus, even a grocery store. I have no car, and I get around well enough on my own."

Q "Public transportation is there, but **it's useless because everyone drives**."

The College Prowler Take On...
Transportation

Most SMU students have only seen the Mustang Express or DART bus; many have never actually been on one. This campus is car oriented—everyone has a car or has befriended someone with one. There are students that use public transportation to get around Dallas or to commute, but most of them complain about the tiresome bus schedules, especially if they are running late and need to get to class on time. The services are readily available; however, students would rather ask their friend for a lift to the airport or take an inexpensive shuttle.

Once you have become acquainted with the bus system (prepare a back-up plan), traveling around town is not extremely mind-boggling. It is a pain to stand at the bus stop in the blistering heat or unbearable cold, and the bus as well as the stations can be pretty sketchy—so befriend someone with a reliable car.

C-

The College Prowler® Grade on

Transportation: C-

A high grade for Transportation indicates that campus buses, public buses, cabs, and rental cars are readily-available and affordable. Other determining factors include proximity to an airport and the necessity of transportation.

Weather

The Lowdown On...
Weather

Average Temperature:		Average Precipitation:	
Fall:	78 °F	Fall:	3.30 in.
Winter:	58 °F	Winter:	2.24 in.
Spring:	77 °F	Spring:	3.96 in.
Summer:	95 °F	Summer:	2.84 in.

Students Speak Out On...
Weather

> "It's very warm at first, but during the winter it can get into the 40s. Bring a sturdy umbrella, because when it rains, it pours."

Q "It is **very hot and humid** in the summer. Bring only Gucci, Prada, or Burberry high heels and all your other designer clothing. For the cold, bring just a medium all-weather jacket. Definitely bring an umbrella."

Q "**The weather is moderate**. It's hot in the summer and cold in the winter."

Q "The weather is always sunny and hot. **Winters are mild and relatively short**. Be ready for the heat, though."

Q "Texas is pretty hot. But **by the time you get to school in the fall, it cools down**. Bring warm clothing for the fall semester, and by mid-way through spring semester, it's warm again. Texas is notoriously unpredictable when it comes to rain and storms."

Q "It's hot, especially in August. **November through February are lovely, and it rarely goes below 40**. You will not need a heavy coat. At night, you'll need to wear gloves, hats, and scarves only a handful of times."

Q "The weather is usually pretty nice here. **It gets extremely hot during the summertime**, though. It usually snows once a year, too. Dallas has great all-around weather. Bring all types of clothes."

Q "It is intensely humid here during the summer, cool and windy during the fall, fairly cold during the winter with **slushy snow every now and then**, and during the spring it's very pleasant."

Q "**The weather is always changing**, so be prepared for anything."

Q "**Expect hot Texas weather**. But everyone here dresses in high school fashions, so make sure to bring all of your designer labels, for you will be judged by them."

Q "The weather is all over the place. Bring some of everything from way hot to way cold. **A waterproof windbreaker is a must**. Bring costume stuff, because it's fun, and most parties are themed. Bring your own clothes and style. There are the Gucci decked heel wearers, but at the same time, flip-flop, jeans, and T-shirt wearers, too."

Q "The weather changes everyday. It's typically hot and humid, but it rains a lot in November, and it gets really cold in January and February. **It has snowed for at least two days in February every year I've been here**."

Q "The weather is mostly warm, but don't forget your umbrella. Many freshmen get soaked during the first downpour of the year. **Don't be surprised if one day it's 70 degrees outside, and the next day it's snowing and there is no class**."

Q "**Prepare for humidity and hail**. It can go from 50 to 90 in a matter of hours. I am not joking. Bring everything. It is the strangest weather I have ever experienced."

Q "The weather is very hot most of the time. During the winter, you will need a coat and jeans because **it does get cold in Texas**. Now, snow is a different thing—it doesn't really happen."

The College Prowler Take On...
Weather

The rumors are true . . . it's hot in Texas! Dallas weather varies by month, but the trends tend to remain constant. Upon arrival to campus in August, people wear shorts, mini-skirts, flip-flops, tank tops, and anything that allows for breathing room from the awful humidity. The sun continues to beat its massive rays down on SMU until a random day when the raindrops fall out of nowhere. Many people are fooled by the sun and never expect rain. Invest in a sturdy umbrella, rain boots, and rain jackets. The rain may continue on for days—or only minutes—before the sun is visible again. As the winter and fall months begin, students transition into wearing jeans more often, as well as sweaters, SMU hoodies, Juicy velour suits, Ugg boots, heels, Birkenstocks, sneakers, and anoraks. Towards the end of February, as the coldest months come to a close, flip-flops are retrieved once again.

Dallas has every type of weather imaginable. But between the end of January and the middle of February, expect a day or two of snow. Although it may only be an inch or two, the administration may cancel classes depending on how icy the roads are. Be prepared to park your car in the garage because hail is always a possibility. Also, bring bug repellant! Mosquitoes are in full force during August and September. If you choose to remain in Dallas during the summer, be prepared for a high electric bill because it gets very hot and humid. This state has the most sporadic weather, so you just never know.

B-

The College Prowler® Grade on
Weather: B-

A high Weather grade designates that temperatures are mild and rarely reach extremes, that the campus tends to be sunny rather than rainy, and that weather is fairly consistent rather than unpredictable.

Report Card Summary

B+
ACADEMICS

B+
GUYS

A-
LOCAL ATMOSPHERE

A
GIRLS

B-
SAFETY & SECURITY

C+
ATHLETICS

C+
COMPUTERS

A-
NIGHTLIFE

C
FACILITIES

A-
GREEK LIFE

C+
CAMPUS DINING

C-
DRUG SCENE

A
OFF-CAMPUS DINING

B
CAMPUS STRICTNESS

B
CAMPUS HOUSING

D
PARKING

B+
OFF-CAMPUS HOUSING

C-
TRANSPORTATION

C-
DIVERSITY

B-
WEATHER

Overall Experience

Overall Experience

"SMU is great for some, but not for others. If you are from out-of-state, you won't like it because Texans love Texas, and outsiders may not. But this is from my experience. I would rather be on the East Coast."

Q "I wish I was in a more crowded area like New York, where people are more open and don't mind diversity."

Q "I am generally pleased with the school. I think that had I not chosen my specific major (dance), I would have liked to go somewhere a little smaller, a little closer to home, and a little less Greek."

Q "Even though I hate the frats, and our football team sucks, **I have made so many friends here**. The faculty in Dedman have helped me do so much that I can't imagine being anywhere else. Besides that, the fact that so many guys at our school act like total tools just increases my chance with some of the hottest and richest women in the United States."

Q "My experience has been good. **SMU is a place where you can make your personality fit**. You can schedule your classes to be very challenging, and go after an advanced degree or double major. You can be really involved in the social scene and be in all the clubs you want. You can tailor your experience to fit the lifestyle you want, and that is what college should be about."

Q "I don't really wish I was somewhere else. **I have had an excellent experience at SMU**. I've found so many great people and organizations here. I've enjoyed the Texas environment, and the people here are generally a lot friendlier than the people of the coast cities. It's just a great place, especially the area. If you were only on campus, you would never know that there is a huge city out there. SMU is its own little paradise in the middle of Dallas. I really like this school. There's something for everyone, and there are people coming from all walks of life here. There's a student organization for everyone."

Q "I don't wish I was somewhere else. I've loved my SMU experience. **I've made friends here that I will have for the rest of my life**. Hopefully, this school will help me get a good job in the future. SMU was my accidental last minute school, and I ended up getting a lot of scholarship money, so I came. But I'm glad I did."

Q "**I love this school**. It provides a great place to find out who I am. I love all sorts of people, and most of the kids are cool here, even though most of them are caught up in the high society game."

Q "I think Dallas and the school offer so much, no matter what you are into. Dallas has great concerts, good bars, and a friendly community. The campus is beautiful (when there is no construction), safe, and **most importantly, a great place to learn**."

Q "I like it, but **I do wish I was somewhere that wasn't so conservative**."

Q "I think it has been great. There are always things and people you don't like, but **the good far surpasses the bad**. Everyone has some low moments. Sophomore blues set in during second semester of sophomore year, and that's rough. But that's to be expected. I look forward to going back each semester, as I realize how lucky I am to be getting an education, let alone at the school I want to go to. I can't see myself elsewhere or without the fabulous friends I've made."

Q "I think it's a great school. I've made great friends and had a lot of fun. However, it is kind of hard, because **I've found that a lot of people transfer after a year or two**."

Q "**At first, you may not like SMU—but give it time** because you will really enjoy it later on."

Q "I picked SMU out of a hat basically. It had everything I wanted: small and private with a Greek system, but also large enough to meet new people in every class. **I have never once pictured myself anywhere else**. I absolutely love it, as do all of my very best friends."

Q "My overall experience has been pretty good. I do wish that I would have known about the kind of people that end up going to this school—but I have found some 'diamonds' in this place. **Just realize what you are getting into before you come here**."

Q "I had an incredible time while I was on campus freshman year. I got really involved and jumped right in. That is the best way to have a good time—just immerse yourself. After I moved off campus, and classes started to get harder, I had to pull out of a lot of activities. Therefore, the quality of my experience has gone downhill. Sometimes I do wish I was somewhere else, **maybe the northeast because I am a liberal, but I haven't acted on it**."

Q "**I thought about transferring the first two years I was here**. In the beginning, I felt completely out of my comfort zone here. Being from California, this is just a whole different atmosphere. The people are very similar, but there is a much more laid-back attitude in California. There's a lot less that separates people from classes in California than here. With the exception of big-time college sports, my college experience has been great because I got to get away from home."

Q "I love it. **I would have liked to experience college at a bigger, more normal school**, with more diversity and people. But the education I'm getting here is priceless."

The College Prowler Take On...
Overall Experience

While some SMU students will gladly tell you that this school was their first choice, there are plenty of others that will admit that they're not sure how they got here. For several, SMU was a last-minute decision that turned into a remarkable one. SMU offers individual schools and majors that are praised nationwide. Students are able to test several interests before choosing a particular major. While there are many other things to brag about, like the study abroad programs, the social scene is a key aspect of SMU. This school offers introverts an environment where they can become extroverts in a small community that fosters socializing. Among the community, students get the hookups for internships and jobs by networking with friends and alumni.

An exuberant school spirit in terms of athletics might be missing, but SMU pride in the sense of academic excellence and social atmosphere is highly evident. Students get irritated with parking and other little issues, but in the long run, most of them are satisfied with their level of education and their experience. The majority of students will tell you it has been the best four years of their lives and that they are glad to have stumbled upon such a rare treasure.

The Inside Scoop

The Lowdown On...
The Inside Scoop

SMU Slang:

Know the slang, know the school. The following is a list of things you really need to know before coming to SMU. The more of these words you know, the better off you'll be.

BIC – The Business Information Center.

Boaz Hoes – A nickname applied to all females that live in the Boaz Residence Hall.

The Boulevard – The SMU Boulevard is where tailgating takes place before every football game.

Cinco – The Cinco Center (gym).

Cockintosh – A name for Cockrell-McIntosh Hall.

First-Year – Also known as freshmen. SMU prefers not to call them freshmeat or freshmen.

Fratastic – A term applied to males that are dressed preppy.

GDI – Gosh Darn Independent. This term is used to refer to people who chose not to pledge a fraternity or sorority.

Hughes-Trigg – The Hughes-Trigg Student Center.

Meadows – Referred to as Meadows by all the arts students, it is listed as the Owen Fine Arts Center.

MRS – Students joke that the girls come here to get their "Mrs." degree.

Mustang – Each student is an SMU Mustang.

The North Quad – This section of campus includes Dallas Hall, Fondren, Shuttles, Mary Hay, Peyton, and Virginia-Snider.

Residence Hall – Also referred to as dorms, SMU calls them residence halls.

The SAC – The Student Activities Center is located on the third floor of Hughes-Trigg.

Shacklevany – Another name for McElvaney Hall (students are said to "shack-up" there).

Shittles – Another name for Shuttles Hall.

The South Quad – This section of campus includes McElvaney, Morrison-McGinnis, Meadows Museum of Art, and Cockrell-McIntosh.

Things I Wish I Knew Before Coming to SMU

- It's located in a highly-materialistic social setting.
- It's big on Greek life.
- If you have to take a foreign language, get it all done in the same year.
- It's a party school.
- There is a GPA requirement for the business school.
- It's not very racially diverse.
- Bring bug repellant to annihilate those mosquitoes.
- The overall city does not cater to college students.
- No one goes to any of the athletic events.

Tips to Succeed at SMU

- Ask around about professors before scheduling your classes.
- Don't schedule an 8 a.m. class unless you can definitely get up for it.
- Go to class, especially if there is an attendance policy.
- Befriend the TAs.
- Check your Webmail every day.
- Make sure your teacher knows your name.
- Don't blow off school for parties.
- Keep yourself busy—get involved or pick a minor.
- Take care of all your GEC courses first before your major classes so you can have more time to decide on a major.
- Remember what you're here for!

SMU Urban Legends

- If you step on the University Seal in Dallas Hall, you won't graduate.
- *Playboy* ranked SMU among the top 10 party schools in the nation.
- Sorority girls do more drugs.
- SMU: Southern Millionaires University; obviously, this is not true—there is only a very small percentage of students that even fit into that category.

School Spirit

Students may not be able to recite and sing the "Pony Battle Cry," but they can tell you about several of the top programs in the nation and how worthwhile it is to attend SMU. School spirit may be mediocre most of the time, but after SMU wins a football game, there are cheery faces all over campus for quite a while. The milestone for most people is that SMU has won at least one game. Slowly but steadily, SMU is on its way to possible mediocrity in terms of football, however, school spirit needs to rise a few notches. Students are proud to say that they attend SMU when applying for internships and jobs because the name bears more than athletic apathy. Nothing can stop SMU students from gathering to celebrate; this is evident in most of the large social events on campus.

Traditions

Celebration of Lights

One night during the first week of December, students gather in the Main Quad to participate in the Celebration of Lights, which is a candlelight ceremony of holiday songs and readings. The trees surrounding Dallas Hall, and the building itself, are all illuminated with Christmas lights. Administrators and other guests make abbreviated speeches on the steps of Dallas Hall. There is a small choir and band on the steps, too.

Mane Event

In the spring, the Student Foundation puts on a gigantic festival in front of Dallas Hall, called Mane Event, where students can relax and take a break from studying. SMU does not have a carnival, but this would be the equivalent to it. There is a live band, tons of food, games, and other things to do, such as a moonwalk.

Rotunda Passage

Every freshman has the chance to participate in the Rotunda Passage, which leads to Convocation. It marks a student's official start and end of their SMU college experience. Every year, as a new freshman class, the students gather and walk through the front doors of Dallas Hall. When they graduate, as a senior class, they walk through the Dallas Hall Rotunda again. Along the sidewalks on the way to the Dallas Hall, students hold flags that represent every country and state with a student in that class.

Homecoming

This is an entire weekend devoted to school spirit. First, there is a kickoff party at Hughes-Trigg to mark the beginning of Homecoming. This is also where the candidates for homecoming are introduced. A couple days later, there is a Homecoming Parade, where student organizations present floats they have created. Tailgating follows the parade, and then on to the homecoming football game—where the king and queen are announced.

Mustang Corral

The weekend before school begins, over fifty percent of the incoming freshmen class gather for a weekend retreat in the Texas Hill Country. The entire weekend is guided by faculty, alumni, and student leaders. There are information sessions, games, dances, and much more. It is an introduction to school spirit and camaraderie. This is a great way for the students to bond with their peers before settling in on campus.

Family Weekend and Mother's/Father's Weekend

Family Weekend is designated for the fall, whereas Mother's or Father's Weekend (it switches every spring) takes place in the spring. To start Family Weekend, on Friday night there is a "Talent Show" in McFarlin Auditorium where student organizations perform. Tailgating and a football game occur the next day, as well as several other events for parents and students to participate in. For Mother's/Father's Weekend, there is an annual show called "Sing Song" where student organizations compete against each other by presenting their skits to an audience and judges. The following day is filled with things to do, just like Family Weekend.

Pony Ears

Formed by putting two fingers up in the air and slightly bending them down like ears (no not horns), "pony ears" is SMU's well-known sign. At football games, students can be seen with their pony ears high in the air to show some school spirit.

Brown Bag

Every semester, the dance department showcases student-choreographed pieces in the Bob Hope lobby. Students come for an hour, bring their own "brown bag" lunch, sit on the floor directly in front of the dancers, and watch the show.

Week of Welcome

The week that classes begin, freshmen enjoy a week of fun events. The first day is usually a Sunday when the students are returning from Mustang and moving into their residence halls. That same night, there is an outdoor movie. Monday features a Mustang Mixer and the first-year pictures. A road trip to Six Flags consumes most of Tuesday until the Hypnotist performs in the evening. Finally, the last day before class, there is an Activities Fair and the Rotunda Passage.

First Weekend/Mustang Stampede

This is the first weekend after the initial week of classes. There is a giant barbeque for the entire University, and a comedian that performs later on that night. In the past, SMU has hosted Jamie Kennedy and Jim Breuer. There is a party on Saturday until the wee hours of the morning, and on Sunday, the first University worship celebration is held in the South Quad.

Finding a Job or Internship

The Lowdown On...
Finding a Job or Internship

The Lowdown
Don't lose too much sleep over whether or not you will be able to get a job or internship. The Hegi Family Career Development Center, located in Hughes-Trigg, is looking out for you, but don't forget that most people acquire their jobs and internships through connections and networking.

Advice
During sophomore year, once you have declared your major, stop by the Career Center and get to know your advisor for your specific major. Become familiar with the internship and job listings posted by employers and SMU on MustangTRAK. Figure out what specifics you are looking for, because when the time comes to apply, it is easier to narrow your search. Attend the Career Fair and all other related workshops.

Career Center Resources & Services

Career Assessment

Career Counseling

Career Exploration

Career Fairs

Career Oriented Workshops

Cover Letters and Resume Critiques

Employer Research

Graduate School Advising

Interviewing Resources

Mock Interviews

MustangTRAK

Portfolio Preparation

Average Salary Information

The statistics below represent the average salaries for SMU graduates. The results are from a 2000 survey done by *Forbes* magazine. Not all schools and majors are listed.

Cox School of Business

Marketing	$36,537
Management Information Systems	$39,500
General Business	$41,402
Finance & Financial Consulting	$42,897
Accounting	$44,695
Real Estate Finance	$47,000
Organizational Behavior/Bus. Policy	$49,500

School of Engineering

Engineering Management	$44,000
Information Systems	$44,000
Computer Science	$52,000
Electrical Engineering	$52,000
Mechanical Engineering	$54,000

Firms that Most Frequently Hire Graduates

Accenture, Chase, Deloitte & Touche, JP Morgan, KPMG

Alumni

The Lowdown On...
Alumni

Web Site:
www.smu.edu/alumni

Office:
SMU Office of
Alumni Relations
P.O. Box 750173
Dallas, TX 75272-0173
smualum@mail.smu.edu
(214) 768-2586 or
(888) 327-3755

Services Available:
Affinity/Special
Interest Groups
Alumni Chapters
Alumni Directory
Career Network
Class Notes (updates
on alumni)
E-mail forwarding
Lifelong Learning
Travel Program

Major Alumni Events

Alumni are present at SMU events throughout the year, but the most popular alumni events are tailgating, Homecoming, game days, class reunions, and 50-year reunions. The dates and times for each of these can be found online.

Alumni Publications

SMU Magazine

SMU publishes a quarterly magazine that gives updates on what some of SMU's alumni are currently doing, discusses issues on campus, provides details on upcoming events on campus, and lists alumni that have passed away.

Did You Know?

Famous SMU Alumni

Kathy Bates – Academy Award winning actress

Powers Boothe – Emmy Award winner and star of HBO's *Deadwood*

Laura Bush – First Lady

James Cronin – Nobel Prize winning physicist

Paige Davis – Actress and host of *Trading Spaces*

Robert Dennard – Computer memory pioneer

Eric Dickenson – NFL Hall of Fame

Lars Frolander – Olympic gold medalist

Lauren Graham – Star on TV show *Gilmore Girls*

Beth Henley – Pulitzer Prize winning playwright

Karen Hughes – Special Advisor to President George Bush

Steve Lundquist – Olympic gold medalist

Patricia Richardson – Star on TV show *Home Improvement*

Aaron Spelling – TV producer

Payne Stewart – Champion golfer

Doak Walker – SMU football player, Heisman Trophy recipient

Student Organizations

Advertising Club - *http://people.smu.edu/adclub*

Alliance of Minority Communicators

Alpha Epsilon Delta/Health Prof. Society - *http://people.smu.edu/aed*

Alpha Iota Delta

Alpha Kappa Psi - *http://people.smu.edu/akpsi*

Alpha Lambda Delta - *http://people.smu.edu/ald*

Alpha Phi Omega - *http://people.smu.edu/apo*

American Civil Liberties Union

American Society of Mechanical Engineers - *http://www.engr.smu.edu/orgs/ASME*

Amnesty International

Anthropology Club - *http://people.smu.edu/anthroclub*

Asian American Leadership and Education Conference

Asian Christian Fellowship

Asian Council - *http://people.smu.edu/ac*

Association of Black Students

BACCHUS - a peer support group that provides support and referral to other alcohol and drug programs

Baha'i Club

Baptist Student Ministry

Baseball Club - *http://people.smu.edu/baseball*

Best Buddies

Beta Alpha Psi - *http://people.smu.edu/beta*

Big Brother/Big Sister

Black Law Students Association

Bringing Sisters Together - *http://www.geocities.com/bringingsisterstogether*

Business School Student Caucus

Campus Crusade for Christ - *http://people.smu.edu/crusade*

Campus Ministry Council

Canterbury House - *www.smu.edu/canterbury*

Catholic Campus Ministry - *http://people.smu.edu/ccm*

Chemistry Society

Chi Alpha Christian Fellowship

Chinese Club

Chinese Student Association

Chinese Student Union

Christ Lutheran Church - *http://clcdallas.org*

Christian Brotherhood

Christian Legal Society

Christian Science College Organization

Church of Jesus Christ of Latter-Day Saints

Classical Studies Club

College Hispanic American Students

College Republicans - *http://people.smu.edu/republicans*

Cox MBA Diversity Association

Cycling Club - *http://recsports.smu.edu*

Debate and Forensics Science

Dedman College Student Graduate Assembly

Delta Sigma Pi (Business)

Diabetes Association

Diversity Education Program

East Asian Student Association - *http://people.smu.edu/easa*

Economics Club

Energy Club

Environmental Society

Eta Kappa Nu

Fellowship of Christian Athletes

Finance Investments/Accounting Club (Beta Alpha Psi)

First Year Council

French Club

Gamma Sigma Alpha

Gay, Lesbian, and Bisexual Student Organization - *http://people.smu.edu/glbso*

Geology Club

German Club

Global Connections

Golden Gavel (Legal Honorary)

Golden Key National Honor Society

Graduate Council

Graduate Economics Club

Green Party

He Is Sufficient

Higher Ground

Highland Park Presbyterian Church College Ministry

Highland Park United Methodist Church Class

Hillel/Jewish Students Organization - *http://people.smu.edu/hillel*

Hindu Students Organization

Honor Council

Ice Hockey Club

I-EEE

Interfraternity Council (IFC)

International Association of Business Communicators - *http://people.smu.edu/iabc*

International Relations Club

Intramurals - *http://recsports.smu.edu*

Italian Club

Japan Club

Judo Club - *http://people.smu.edu/judo*

Korean Students Association

Leadership Consultant Council

Lacrosse Club (Men's) - *http://people.smu.edu/lacrosse*

Manada Wranglers

Marketing Club

MBA Consulting Club - *http://people.smu.edu/mbaconsult*

MBA Finance Association - *http://people.smu.edu/mba_finance*

MBA Gay and Lesbian Student Association

MBA Student Council

Meadows Graduate Council

Meadows Student Senate

Men's Soccer

Men's Volleyball Club

Metro Mustangs

Mobilization of Volunteer Efforts (MOVE) - *http://people.smu.edu/move*

Multicultural Greek Council - *www.smugreeks.com*

Mu Phi Epsilon - *http://people.smu.edu/muphi*

Music Educators National Conference

Muslim Student Association - *http://people.smu.edu/msa*

Mustang Cricket Club

Mustang Link

Mustang Marathon - *http://mustangmarathon.com*

Mustang Ropers

Mustangs for Christ

National Pan-Hellenic Council - *http://www.smugreeks.com*

National Society of Black Engineers

National Society of Collegiate Scholars - *http://www.nscs.org*

Non-Traditional Students Organization (SOTA)

Panhellenic Council - *http://www.smugreeks.com*

Perkins Student Association

Persian Student Society - *http://people.smu.edu/isa*

Peruna Productions

Phi Alpha Delta (Pre-Law)

Phi Beta Kappa - *http://people.smu.edu/phi_beta_kappa*

Philosophy Club

Phi Theta Kappa - *http://people.smu.edu/ptk*

Ping Pong Club

Pi Tau Sigma

Political Science Symposium

Program Council

Psi Chi

Radio Television News Director Association (RTNDA)

Racquetball Club

Reformed University Fellowship - *http://www.rufsmu.com*

ReJOYce in Jesus Ministries

Residence Hall Association

Rock Climbing Club

Rugby Football Club

Russian Club

Sailing Club

School of Engineering Graduate Council - *http://seniorgift. smu.edu*

Senior Class Council - *http://seniorgift.smu.edu*

Sigma Rho Delta

Sigma Tau Delta/English Club

SMU Amateur Radio Club

SMU Badminton Club

SMU Ballroom Dance Club - *http://people.smu.edu/ballroom*

SMU Boxing Club

SMU Democrats

SMU Ducks Unlimited

SMU Graduate Rugby Football - *http://recsports.smu.edu*

SMUligans

SMU Medieval Club

SMU Men's Crew - *http://people.smu.edu/crew*

SMU Society for Enterprise Information Technology

SMU Sports Club

SMU S.T.A.N.G.S.

SMU Student Senate - *http://people.smu.edu/senate*

Society of Automotive Engineers - *http://www.engr.smu.edu/ org/minibaja*

Society of Physics Students - *http://www.physics.smu.edu/ ~scalise/SPS*

Society of Professional Journalists

Society of Women Engineers

South Asian Sisterhood Integrating Culture

Spanish Club

Student Association for Music Therapy

Student Athletic Advisory Committee

Student Bar Association

Student Engineers Joint Council

Student Filmmakers Association - *http://people.smu.edu/sfa*

Student Foundation

Student Media Company – *http://smu-dailycampus.com*

Tau Beta Pi

Theta Tau - *http://people.smu.edu/thetatau*

Turkish Students Association - *http://people.smu.edu/tsa*

Undergraduate Economics Club

UNISEF

Victory Campus Ministries

Vietnamese Student Association

Voices of Inspiration Gospel Choir

Water Polo

Wesley Foundation - *http://people.smu.edu/wesley*

Woman's Interest Network (WIN)

Women in Business

Women in Law

Women in Science and Engineering

Women's Volleyball Club

YMCA of SMU

Young Life - *http://www.younglifenorthtexas.org*

The Best
& Worst

The Ten BEST Things About SMU

1	Small classes and teachers that know your name
2	Tailgating
3	Brown Bag in Meadows
4	Study abroad program
5	Tate Lecture Series
6	Local SMU bar specials
7	The attractive campus
8	Sunny weather
9	Greek life
10	Flex Dollars on your meal plan

The Ten **WORST** Things About SMU

1	Parking
2	The Cinco Center
3	Ongoing construction
4	Overwhelmingly conservative
5	Desolate stands during soccer and football games
6	Community bathrooms
7	Greek life
8	Easy to get stuck in the SMU bubble
9	Not as diverse as it could be
10	Low school spirit

Visiting

The Lowdown On...
Visiting

Hotel Information:

The Bradford at Lincoln Park

www.bradfordsuites.com

8221 N. Central Expressway
Dallas, TX 75225

(214) 696-1555

Distance from campus:
3.5 miles

Price Range: $89 (SMU rate)

Courtyard by Marriott

http://marriott.com/default.mi

10325 N. Central Expressway
Dallas, TX 75231

(214) 739-2500

Distance from campus:
4 miles

Price Range: $79 (SMU rate)

Doubletree–Campbell Center
www.doubletree.com
8250 N. Central Expressway
Dallas, TX 75206
(214) 691-8700
Distance from campus:
2.5 miles
Price Range: $129–$154

Embassy Suites–Love Field
www.embassysuites.com
3880 West
Northwest Highway
Dallas, TX 75220
(214) 357-4500
Distance from campus:
6 miles
Price Range: $105 (SMU rate)

Hilton Park Cities
www.hilton.com
5954 Luther Lane
Dallas, TX 75225
(214) 368-0400
Distance from campus:
4.5 miles
Price Range: $99 (SMU rate)

Holiday Inn Select–Central
www.holiday-inn.com
10650 N. Central Expressway
US 75/LBJ
Dallas, TX 75231
(214) 373-6000
Distance from campus:
4.5 miles
Price Range: $64 (SMU rate)

Holiday Inn Select–Love Field
www.holiday-inn.com
3300 West Mockingbird Lane
Dallas, TX 75235
(214) 357-8500
Distance from campus:
Less than 4 miles
Price Range: $79 (SMU rate)

The Melrose Hotel
www.melrosehoteldallas.com
3015 Oak Lawn Avenue
Dallas, TX 75219
(214) 521-5151
Distance from campus:
Less than 4 miles
Price Range: $189 (walk-in),
$159 (reservation)

The Radisson

www.radisson.com

6060 N. Central Expressway
Dallas, TX 75206

(214) 750-6060

Distance from campus:
Less than a mile

Price Range: $84 (SMU rate)

**Wyndham Garden–
Dallas Park Central**

www.wyndham.com

8051 LBJ Freeway
Dallas, TX 75251

(972) 680-3000

Distance from campus: Less
than 9 miles

Price Range: $64–$84

Take a Campus Virtual Tour

www.smu.edu/admission/virtualsmu.asp

To Schedule a Group Information Session or Interview

Call 1-800-323-0672 or (214) 768-2058 on any weekday
from 8:30 a.m.–5 p.m., and on some select Saturdays from
9:30 a.m.–noon.

The admission staff conducts tours regularly Monday–Friday
every week, however, certain tours close until the fall semester
(the Residence Hall tour). Check the Web site for specific days
that feature a 10 a.m.–3 p.m. tour and an overnight tour.

Campus Tours

Tours are normally conducted every weekday, except for posted days and Mustang Mondays. The tours begin at 10 a.m., and the last tour is at 3 p.m. The day includes two information sessions, two campus tours, a residence hall tour, and lunch. Call to schedule a tour in advance.

Parade Reviews

Prospective students have the chance to find out what it's like to go to SMU for one night. They stay with an assigned student in a residence hall overnight, and tour the school the next day. This option is only available Sunday through Thursday evenings. Allow two week's notice to the school if you would like to participate in this program.

If you're interested in getting to know the campus a bit better, call the Division of Enrollment Services at (214) 768-2058 to reserve a spot.

Once you have received your acceptance packet, SMU will invite you to attend Mustang Days, where you have the chance to stay for an entire weekend and become better acquainted with the campus, the professors, the administrators, and students.

By no means will these overnight visits give you complete insight into the school—so learn as much as you can in the minimal amount of time you have. Play twenty questions with your host, bring this book, and grill any students that have the time to talk with you.

Directions to Campus

Driving from the North

- Go south on IH-35E to exit East IH-635 (LBJ Freeway).
- Exit 75-South (North Central Expressway) towards Dallas.
- Continue on 75-South and exit Lovers Lane.
- Stay on service road and turn right on SMU Boulevard.
- At the intersection of SMU Boulevard and Airline Road, park in the Moody Parking Garage.

Driving from the South

- Go north on IH-35E and exit east onto Woodall Rogers Freeway.
- Get in the far left lane and exit 75-North (North Central Expressway) towards Sherman.
- Continue driving and exit Mockingbird Lane.
- Stay on the service road and turn left on SMU Boulevard.
- At the intersection of SMU Boulevard and Airline Road, park in the Moody Parking Garage.

Driving from the East

- Take IH-30 west and exit 75-North (North Central Expressway).
- Continue north and exit Mockingbird Lane.
- Stay on the service road and turn left on SMU Boulevard.
- At the intersection of SMU Boulevard and Airline Road, park in the Moody Parking Garage.

Driving from the West (D/FW Airport)

- Take the north exit of the airport.
- Get on IH-635 east and continue to 75-South (North Central Expressway) towards downtown.
- Continue driving and exit Lovers Lane.
- Stay on the service road and turn right onto SMU Boulevard. At the intersection of SMU Boulevard and Airline Road, park in the Moody Parking Garage.

Words to Know

Academic Probation – A suspension imposed on a student if he or she fails to keep up with the school's minimum academic requirements. Those unable to improve their grades after receiving this warning can face dismissal.

Beer Pong/Beirut – A drinking game involving cups of beer arranged in a pyramid shape on each side of a table. The goal is to get a ping pong ball into one of the opponent's cups by throwing the ball or hitting it with a paddle. If the ball lands in a cup, the opponent is required to drink the beer.

Bid – An invitation from a fraternity or sorority to 'pledge' (join) that specific house.

Blue-Light Phone – Brightly-colored phone posts with a blue light bulb on top. These phones exist for security purposes and are located at various outside locations around most campuses. In an emergency, a student can pick up one of these phones (free of charge) to connect with campus police or a security escort.

Campus Police – Police who are specifically assigned to a given institution. Campus police are typically not regular city officers; they are employed by the university in a full-time capacity.

Club Sports – A level of sports that falls somewhere between varsity and intramural. If a student is unable to commit to a varsity team but has a lot of passion for athletics, a club sport could be a better, less intense option. Even less demanding, intramural (IM) sports often involve no traveling and considerably less time.

Cocaine – An illegal drug. Also known as "coke" or "blow," cocaine often resembles a white crystalline or powdery substance. It is highly addictive and dangerous.

Common Application – An application with which students can apply to multiple schools.

Course Registration – The period of official class selection for the upcoming quarter or semester. Prior to registration, it is best to prepare several back-up courses in case a particular class becomes full. If a course is full, students can place themselves on the waitlist, although this still does not guarantee entry.

Division Athletics – Athletic classifications range from Division I to Division III. Division IA is the most competitive, while Division III is considered to be the least competitive.

Dorm – A dorm (or dormitory) is an on-campus housing facility. Dorms can provide a range of options from suite-style rooms to more communal options that include shared bathrooms. Most first-year students live in dorms. Some upperclassmen who wish to stay on campus also choose this option.

Early Action – An application option with which a student can apply to a school and receive an early acceptance response without a binding commitment. This system is becoming less and less available.

Early Decision – An application option that students should use only if they are certain they plan to attend the school in question. If a student applies using the early decision option and is admitted, he or she is required and bound to attend that university. Admission rates are usually higher among students who apply through early decision, as the student is clearly indicating that the school is his or her first choice.

Ecstasy – An illegal drug. Also known as "E" or "X," ecstasy looks like a pill and most resembles an aspirin. Considered a party drug, ecstasy is very dangerous and can be deadly.

Ethernet – An extremely fast Internet connection available in most university-owned residence halls. To use an Ethernet connection properly, a student will need a network card and cable for his or her computer.

Fake ID – A counterfeit identification card that contains false information. Most commonly, students get fake IDs with altered birthdates so that they appear to be older than 21 (and therefore of legal drinking age). Even though it is illegal, many college students have fake IDs in hopes of purchasing alcohol or getting into bars.

Frosh – Slang for "freshman" or "freshmen."

Hazing – Initiation rituals administered by some fraternities or sororities as part of the pledging process. Many universities have outlawed hazing due to its degrading and sometimes dangerous nature.

Intramurals (IMs) – A popular, and usually free, sport league in which students create teams and compete against one another. These sports vary in competitiveness, and can include a range of activities—everything from billiards to water polo. IM sports are a great way to meet people with similar interests.

Keg – Officially called a half-barrel, a keg contains roughly 200 12-ounce servings of beer.

LSD – An illegal drug. Also known as acid, this hallucinogenic drug most commonly resembles a tab of paper.

Marijuana – An illegal drug also known as weed or pot. Along with alcohol, marijuana is one of the most commonly-found drugs on campuses across the country.

Major –The focal point of a student's college studies; a specific topic that is studied for a degree. Examples of majors include physics, English, history, computer science, economics, business, and music. Many students decide on a specific major before arriving on campus, while others are simply "undecided" until declaring a major. Those who are extremely interested in two areas can also choose to double major.

Meal Block – The equivalent of one meal. Students on a meal plan usually receive a fixed number of meals per week. Each meal, or "block," can be redeemed at the school's dining facilities in place of cash. Often, a student's weekly allotment of meal blocks will be forfeited if not used.

Minor – An additional focal point in a student's education. Often serving as a complement or addition to a student's main area of focus, a minor has fewer requirements and prerequisites to fulfill than a major. Minors are not required for graduation from most schools; however some students who want to explore many different interests choose to pursue both a major and a minor.

Mushrooms – An illegal drug. Also known as "shrooms," this drug resembles regular mushrooms but is extremely hallucinogenic.

Off-Campus Housing – Housing from a particular landlord or rental group that is not affiliated with the university. Depending on the college, off-campus housing can range from extremely popular to non-existent. Students who choose to live off campus are typically given more freedom, but they also have to deal with possible subletting scenarios, furniture, bills, and other issues. In addition to these factors, rental prices and distance often affect a student's decision to move off campus.

Office Hours – Time that teachers set aside for students who have questions about coursework. Office hours are a good forum for students to go over any problems and to show interest in the subject material.

Pledging – The early phase of joining a fraternity or sorority, pledging takes place after a student has gone through rush and received a bid. Pledging usually lasts between one and two semesters. Once the pledging period is complete and a particular student has done everything that is required to become a member, that student is considered a brother or sister. If a fraternity or a sorority would decide to "haze" a group of students, this initiation would take place during the pledging period.

Private Institution – A school that does not use tax revenue to subsidize education costs. Private schools typically cost more than public schools and are usually smaller.

Prof – Slang for "professor."

Public Institution – A school that uses tax revenue to subsidize education costs. Public schools are often a good value for in-state residents and tend to be larger than most private colleges.

Quarter System (or Trimester System) – A type of academic calendar system. In this setup, students take classes for three academic periods. The first quarter usually starts in late September or early October and concludes right before Christmas. The second quarter usually starts around early to mid–January and finishes up around March or April. The last academic quarter, or "third quarter," usually starts in late March or early April and finishes up in late May or mid-June. The fourth quarter is summer. The major difference between the quarter system and semester system is that students take more, less comprehensive, courses under the quarter calendar.

RA (Resident Assistant) – A student leader who is assigned to a particular floor in a dormitory in order to help the other students who live there. An RA's duties include ensuring student safety and providing assistance wherever possible.

Recitation – An extension of a specific course; a review session. Some classes, particularly large lectures, are supplemented with mandatory recitation sessions that provide a relatively personal class setting.

Rolling Admissions – A form of admissions. Most commonly found at public institutions, schools with this type of policy continue to accept students throughout the year until their class sizes are met. For example, some schools begin accepting students as early as December and will continue to do so until April or May.

Room and Board – This figure is typically the combined cost of a university-owned room and a meal plan.

Room Draw/Housing Lottery – A common way to pick on-campus room assignments for the following year. If a student decides to remain in university-owned housing, he or she is assigned a unique number that, along with seniority, is used to determine his or her housing for the next year.

Rush – The period in which students can meet the brothers and sisters of a particular chapter and find out if a given fraternity or sorority is right for them. Rushing a fraternity or a sorority is not a requirement at any school. The goal of rush is to give students who are serious about pledging a feel for what to expect.

Semester System – The most common type of academic calendar system at college campuses. This setup typically includes two semesters in a given school year. The fall semester starts around the end of August or early September and concludes before winter vacation. The spring semester usually starts in mid-January and ends in late April or May.

Student Center/Rec Center/Student Union – A common area on campus that often contains study areas, recreation facilities, and eateries. This building is often a good place to meet up with fellow students; depending on the school, the student center can have a huge role or a non-existent role in campus life.

Student ID – A university-issued photo ID that serves as a student's key to school-related functions. Some schools require students to show these cards in order to get into dorms, libraries, cafeterias, and other facilities. In addition to storing meal plan information, in some cases, a student ID can actually work as a debit card and allow students to purchase things from bookstores or local shops.

Suite – A type of dorm room. Unlike dorms that feature communal bathrooms shared by the entire floor, suites offer bathrooms shared only among the suite. Suite-style dorm rooms can house anywhere from two to ten students.

TA (Teacher's Assistant) – An undergraduate or grad student who helps in some manner with a specific course. In some cases, a TA will teach a class, assist a professor, grade assignments, or conduct office hours.

Undergraduate – A student in the process of studying for his or her bachelor's degree.

ABOUT THE AUTHOR

Since I was nine, I've enjoyed writing—well mainly about my overeager urge to become a doctor even though I can't stand the sight of blood. Then I took a turn down ballerina lane, reaped the benefits of injuries, and somehow managed to return to my longtime interest in writing. Currently, I am a junior journalism major and a dance minor hoping to find a job where I can utilize my creativity and partake in the freedom of expression. I'm very thankful that I have been given the opportunity to help attract the right students to SMU, as well as offer some advice to the irresolute ones. Getting away from Georgia has been quite an eye-opener for me, and through my college experience, I have learned what the beauty of independence has to offer. I've learned how to juggle school, a job, extracurriculars, and my sanity. Yet somehow, I've managed to have the time of my life here, too. It certainly has been worthwhile for me, and hopefully this book will help you decide whether or not it can be for you, too.

Don't fret, I'm not going to write a novel about myself or anything. I would like to give some shout outs and thank yous to the people who made this book possible. Thank you to my parents, who were there for all of my frantic phone calls. My family rocks! They've all been cheering me on. Thank you to Chris for always hugging me and saying, "you can do it!" Thank you to Kristin Diver, Kristen the German, Jen, Mary B., Sam, Natasha, Prem, Skippy, T. Diddy, Dchizzle, Browns, Penmans, Shumates, Mr. Dealey, Helmuth, and my favorite Texas hotties for all your support. A warm thank you to the College Prowler team, especially Omid! You guys have been so helpful and kind. Thank you again.

Stacy Seebode
stacyseebode@collegeprowler.com

California Colleges

California dreamin'?
This book is a must have for you!

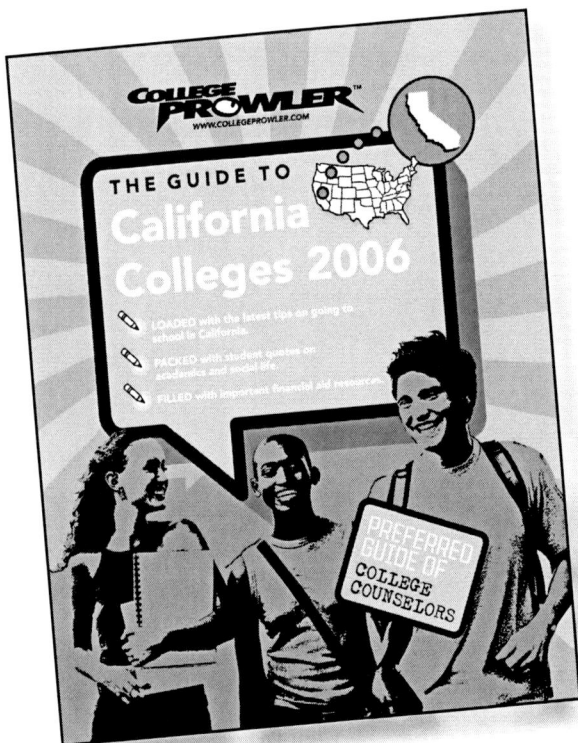

CALIFORNIA COLLEGES
7¼" X 10", 762 Pages Paperback
$29.95 Retail
1-59658-501-3

Stanford, UC Berkeley, Caltech—California is home to some of America's greatest institutes of higher learning. *California Colleges* gives the lowdown on 24 of the best, side by side, in one prodigious volume.

New England Colleges

Looking for peace in the Northeast?
Pick up this regional guide to New England!

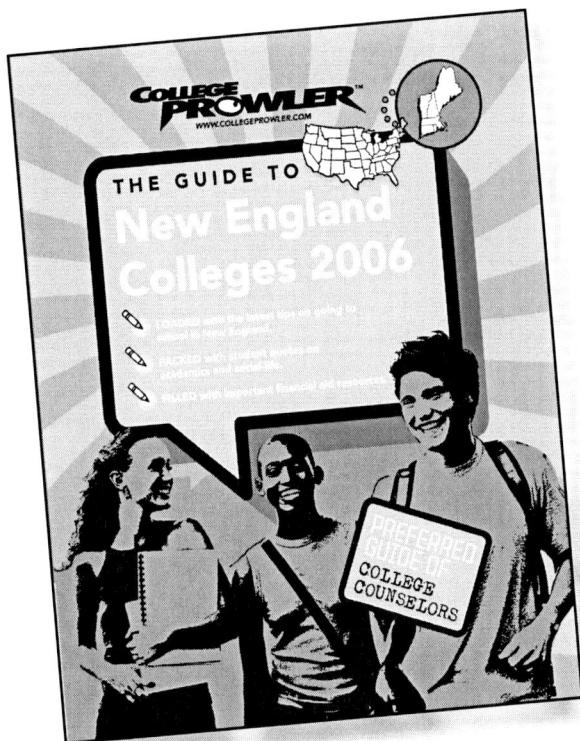

NEW ENGLAND COLLEGES
7¼" X 10", 1015 Pages Paperback
$29.95 Retail
1-59658-504-8

New England is the birthplace of many prestigious universities, and with so many to choose from, picking the right school can be a tough decision. With inside information on over 34 competive Northeastern schools, *New England Colleges* provides the same high-quality information prospective students expect from College Prowler in one all-inclusive, easy-to-use reference.

Schools of the South

Headin' down south? This book will help you find your way to the perfect school!

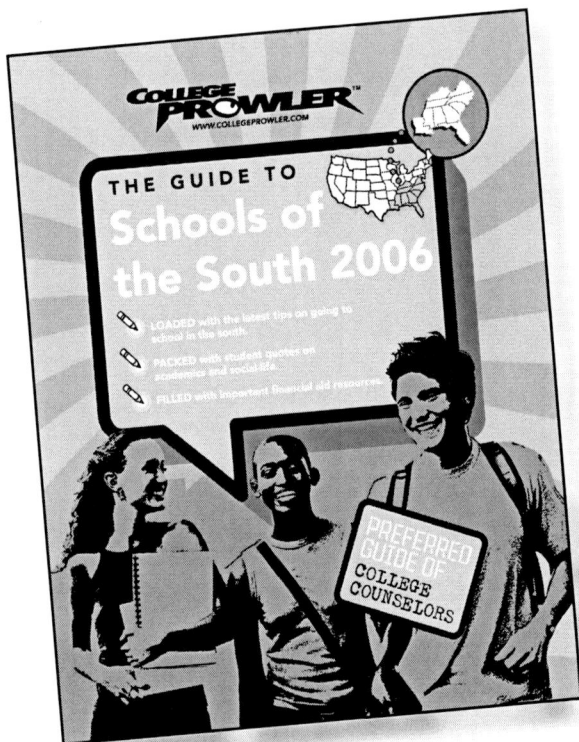

SCHOOLS OF THE SOUTH
7¼" X 10", 773 Pages Paperback
$29.95 Retail
1-59658-503-X

Southern pride is always strong. Whether it's across town or across state, many Southern students are devoted to their home sweet home. *Schools of the South* offers an honest student perspective on 36 universities available south of the Mason-Dixon.

Untangling the Ivy League

The ultimate book for everything Ivy!

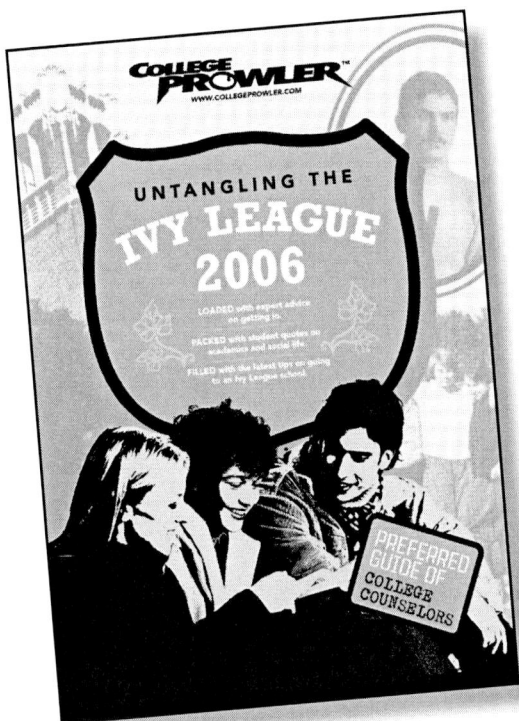

UNTANGLING THE IVY LEAGUE
7¼" X 10", 567 Pages Paperback
$24.95 Retail
1-59658-500-5

Ivy League students, alumni, admissions officers, and other top insiders get together to tell it like it is. *Untangling the Ivy League* covers every aspect—from admissions and athletics to secret societies and urban legends—of the nation's eight oldest, wealthiest, and most competitive colleges and universities.

Tell Us What Life Is Really Like at Your School!

Have you ever wanted to let people know what your college is really like? Now's your chance to help millions of high school students choose the right college.

Let your voice be heard.

Check out *www.collegeprowler.com* for more info!

COLLEGE PROWLER®

Need More Help?

Do you have more questions about this school? Can't find a certain statistic? College Prowler is here to help. We are the best source of college information out there. We have a network of thousands of students who can get the latest information on any school to you ASAP. E-mail us at info@collegeprowler.com with your college-related questions.

E-Mail Us Your College-Related Questions!

Check out *www.collegeprowler.com* for more details.
1-800-290-2682

COLLEGE PROWLER®

Write For Us!
Get published! Voice your opinion.

Writing a College Prowler guidebook is both fun and rewarding; our open-ended format allows your own creativity free reign. Our writers have been featured in national newspapers and have seen their names in bookstores across the country. Now is your chance to break into the publishing industry with one of the country's fastest-growing publishers!

Apply now at ***www.collegeprowler.com***

Contact editor@collegeprowler.com or call 1-800-290-2682 for more details.

COLLEGE PROWLER®

Pros and Cons

Still can't figure out if this is the right school for you?
You've already read through this in-depth guide; why not
list the pros and cons? It will really help with narrowing down
your decision and determining whether or not
this school is right for you.

Pros	Cons
....	....
....	....
....	....
....	....
....	....
....	....
....	....
....	....
....	....
....	....
....	....
....	....
....	....

Pros and Cons

Still can't figure out if this is the right school for you?
You've already read through this in-depth guide; why not
list the pros and cons? It will really help with narrowing down
your decision and determining whether or not
this school is right for you.

Pros	Cons
....	....
....	....
....	....
....	....
....	....
....	....
....	....
....	....
....	....
....	....
....	....
....	....
....	....

Notes

....

....

....

....

....

....

....

....

....

....

....

....

....

COLLEGE PROWLER®

Notes

....

....

....

....

....

....

....

....

....

....

....

....

....

Notes

....

....

....

....

....

....

....

....

....

....

....

....

....